Performance Optimization Made Simple

A Practical Guide to Programming

WILLIAM E. CLARK

Contents

Preface

Performance optimization is a critical concern in software development, affecting application speed, scalability, resource efficiency, and user satisfaction. This book, *Performance Optimization Made Simple: A Practical Guide to Programming*, is designed to provide a comprehensive, accessible introduction to the principles, techniques, and best practices that underpin high-performance software engineering.

The content of this book is structured to guide readers through the foundational aspects of performance, advancing logically from essential concepts to practical implementations. The initial chapters establish the importance of program performance and introduce fundamental terms, ensuring a clear understanding of the optimization landscape. Key performance metrics, program execution stages, and common bottlenecks are examined to lay a solid foundation.

Subsequent chapters methodically address major domains impacting software performance. These include data structure selection, algorithmic complexity, memory management, input/output operations, and the interplay between concurrency, parallelism, and hardware. Dedicated sections provide practical strategies for choosing efficient data structures, evaluating algorithmic efficiency, minimizing memory overhead, and optimizing data transfer.

Profiling, debugging, and systematic testing are explored as essential tools for diagnosing and improving performance. Readers will find guidance on using industry-standard tools and iterative workflows to identify, analyze, and resolve issues. Special considerations for mobile, embedded, and energy-constrained devices are examined, alongside discussions of trade-offs between optimization and security.

Intended for both students and industry professionals, this book does not assume specialized expertise. Readers familiar with the basics of programming—regardless of language—will benefit from the practical examples and actionable advice. Software engineers, system architects, and computer science learners can expect to deepen their understanding of performance optimization and acquire skills applicable across a wide variety of projects and platforms.

By the conclusion of this book, readers will be able to identify performance challenges, select and implement effective optimizations, and sustain high standards of efficiency throughout the software development lifecycle. The material is organized to serve as both a progressive learning resource and a practical reference for optimizing real-world systems.

1

Introduction to Performance Optimization

This chapter emphasizes the importance of program performance in modern software development and daily life, highlighting how efficiency impacts user experience and resource utilization. It introduces key concepts and terms related to optimization, establishing a common vocabulary for the reader. The chapter explains the stages of program execution, from source code to hardware interaction, illustrating where performance issues can arise. It also discusses how to set realistic performance goals based on project constraints and requirements. Lastly, it offers guidance on how to best utilize the book and tailor the learning process to individual needs and interests.

1.1 Why Program Performance Matters

In contemporary software development, program performance represents a critical dimension that affects nearly every aspect of the application lifecycle. Efficiency and speed are no longer optional qualities but fundamental requirements needed to meet user demands and system constraints. As computational complexity rises and software becomes integral to diverse devices and services, the importance of optimizing performance gains prominence. Well-performing software ensures that operations complete promptly, resources are utilized effectively, and the overall system remains responsive under variable conditions.

One primary reason performance is crucial relates to user experience. Software applications that deliver fast response times facilitate smooth interactions, fostering user satisfaction and engagement. When applications respond without perceptible delay, users can focus on their tasks without distraction, improving productivity and increasing the likelihood of continued use. Conversely, slow or lagging software can frustrate users, pushing them toward alternatives. This phenomenon significantly impacts retention in competitive markets, where seamless performance forms part of the expected quality standard.

In addition to enhancing user engagement, program performance directly influences resource consumption. Software applications rely on various underlying resources including the central processing unit (CPU), memory, battery power (particularly for mobile devices), and network bandwidth. Inefficient programs consume excessive CPU cycles, leading to increased heat generation and reduced device lifespan. Programs with large memory footprints risk exhausting available system memory, potentially causing slowdowns or crashes. On battery-powered devices, poorly optimized code accelerates battery depletion, reducing usability and user satisfaction. Meanwhile, network congestion caused by inefficient data transfer imposes latency and can incur financial costs through data charges for users. These considerations are particularly critical in resource-constrained environments such as Internet of Things (IoT) devices, embedded systems, and mobile computing platforms.

Optimizing program performance also bears significant economic implications, especially in large-scale and cloud-based deployments. Efficient code execution reduces the computational load on servers, lowering energy consumption and cooling requirements in data centers. This reduction can translate into measurable cost savings by minimizing the number of active servers required to handle given workloads. Additionally, optimized software often demands less network bandwidth and storage, reducing operational expenses related to data transfer and infrastructure. Organizations that invest in performance tuning therefore gain improved cost efficiency, enabling greater scalability and profitability.

Multiple real-world examples illustrate the tangible impacts of performance shortcomings on popular applications and services. For instance, well-known websites and online platforms have experienced user attrition or revenue declines associated with slow page load times and delayed content delivery. In e-commerce, studies reveal that even small increases in page latency lead to measurable drops in conversion rates, directly affecting sales. Similarly, video streaming services that fail to maintain consistent buffer-free playback experience user dissatisfaction and subscriber churn. These scenarios emphasize how performance issues translate into business risks and lost opportunities when left unaddressed.

Everyday activities rely on software performance to function reliably and efficiently. Navigation applications require rapid computation of optimal routes and real-time traffic updates to guide users effectively. Video streaming platforms depend on sustained data throughput and minimal latency to provide uninterrupted viewing experiences. Online shopping systems must handle large volumes of transactions and inventory queries swiftly to ensure customer satisfaction. Communication tools depend on low-latency message delivery and synchronization to facilitate natural conversations. In all these cases, software performance directly modulates the quality and effectiveness of the services users implicitly expect.

Beyond individual user interactions, program performance serves as a key differentiator in competitive markets. Faster and more efficient applications can offer superior experiences that attract and retain users, fostering brand loyalty and reputation. In sectors where alternatives abound, performance advantages become critical competitive assets. Enterprises that prioritize performance optimization often gain first-mover benefits when launching new features or entering emerging markets. As software ecosystems evolve, performance excellence remains a pillar for sustainable success and innovation leadership.

Focusing on performance also impacts the development and maintenance phases of software projects. While striving for efficient solutions can introduce additional code complexity, it frequently necessitates more rigorous testing to ensure that optimized components behave correctly under diverse conditions. Debugging performance-related issues demands specialized tools and expertise that extend beyond functional correctness. Moreover, maintaining performance over time requires regular profiling and tuning as software evolves and dependencies change. Consequently, performance considerations influence coding standards, testing protocols, and documentation practices, shaping development workflows and long-term maintainability strategies.

Table 1.1: *Key Areas Influenced by Program Performance*

Area	Description
User Experience	Faster response times and smooth interaction increase satisfaction, reduce frustration, and improve retention.
Resource Utilization	Reduced CPU cycles, memory footprint, battery consumption, and bandwidth usage extend device capabilities and system stability.
Economic Efficiency	Lower operational costs through decreased server load, energy usage, and infrastructure demands increase scalability and profitability.
Real-world Impact	Negative performance can reduce revenue, increase churn, and damage brand reputation in competitive environments.
Daily Functionality	Performance affects critical functions such as navigation, streaming, online transactions, and communication reliability.
Competitive Advantage	Efficient software differentiates products and services by providing superior user experiences and enabling innovation.
Development	Performance goals influence code complexity, testing rigor, debugging effort, and sustain long-term software quality.

Collectively, these factors affirm the necessity of prioritizing performance in software engineering practices. The effectiveness of modern software applications hinges on their ability to operate rapidly, efficiently, and reliably within the constraints of their operating environments. Addressing performance from the earliest stages of development reduces downstream risks and costs, creating robust foundations for success. By understanding these fundamental impacts, developers and managers can better appreciate the value of optimization efforts and integrate performance considerations strategically throughout the software lifecycle.

1.2   Overview of Optimization Principles

Performance optimization in software development is the systematic process of improving code to enhance its execution speed and reduce the consumption of computational resources such as memory, processor cycles, and network bandwidth. This improvement aims to make programs run more efficiently while maintaining correctness and reliability. Optimization is not simply about making code faster; it also involves reducing resource usage and balancing multiple competing demands to achieve effective overall system performance within given constraints.

To navigate performance optimization effectively, it is essential to understand fundamental terminology. Latency refers to the time delay between a request and the corresponding response, such as the time a program takes to complete a task or a system to respond to user input. Throughput measures how much work a system can accomplish in a given amount of time, typically expressed as operations per second or transactions per second. Bandwidth relates to the capacity of a communication channel, indicating the amount of data that can be transmitted over a network or bus within one second. Efficiency broadly describes how well a program uses available resources relative to the output it generates. The term bottleneck identifies a component or section of the system whose limited capacity restricts overall performance, acting as a choke point that impairs throughput or increases latency.

Optimization inherently involves trade-offs, and understanding these trade-offs is vital for making balanced decisions. Often, prioritizing speed may increase memory consumption; for instance, caching data to avoid recomputation can reduce execution time but consume more memory. Similarly, reducing memory usage may require more complex algorithms or data access patterns that slow down processing. There is also a trade-off between simplicity and complexity. Simpler code tends to be easier to maintain and less prone to bugs but might not exploit all performance improvements that more complex solutions could achieve. As such, optimization demands careful consideration of project requirements, resource availability, maintainability, and development effort.

A critical concept in performance analysis is the identification of bottlenecks. Bottlenecks occur when a specific resource, such as CPU speed, disk input/output, or network transfer rate, limits the system's capability to perform work efficiently. For example, if a program spends the majority of its time waiting for data to be read from a slow disk, the disk input/output represents a bottleneck. Improving other areas of the program will yield little benefit until the bottleneck is addressed. Thus, pinpointing and alleviating bottlenecks is a fundamental step in optimization to achieve meaningful performance gains.

Measuring performance accurately forms the cornerstone of any optimization effort. Common metrics include response time, which quantifies latency; throughput, referring to the number of operations completed per unit time; and resource utilization, measuring how extensively hardware components are used during execution. Various tools and techniques exist for measuring these metrics, ranging from simple timers inserted around code sections to more sophisticated profilers that analyze CPU and memory usage dynamically. Consistent measurement enables quantitative assessment of improvements and supports informed decision-making.

However, optimization carries costs. Adding performance enhancements can increase code complexity, making software more difficult to read, test, and maintain. Complex optimizations may also introduce subtle bugs or unexpected behavior, requiring additional effort in debugging and quality assurance. Therefore, developers must weigh the benefits of performance improvements against the added complexity, ensuring that optimizations justify their impact on the software lifecycle.

Standard strategies for optimization encompass multiple approaches. Improving algorithms often yields the most significant benefits by reducing the fundamental amount of work required. For example, replacing a naive search algorithm with a more efficient one can drastically reduce running time. Choosing efficient data structures is equally important, as they affect access speed, memory usage, and scalability. Applying caching techniques to store precomputed results or frequently accessed data can minimize redundant computations and reduce latency. Other tactics include minimizing input/output operations, exploiting parallelism, and leveraging hardware-specific features.

The following pseudocode illustrates a common optimization technique targeting algorithmic complexity. Consider the problem of finding an element in a list:

```
# Naive approach: quadratic time complexity O(n^2)
for i in 0 to length(A) - 1:
    count = 0
    for j in 0 to length(A) - 1:
        if A[j] == A[i]:
            count = count + 1
    if count > length(A)/2:
        return A[i]
return null

# Optimized approach: linear time complexity O(n)
candidate = null
count = 0
```

10

```
for element in A:
    if count == 0:
        candidate = element
        count = 1
    else if element == candidate:
        count = count + 1
    else:
        count = count - 1
verify candidate appears more than n/2 times and return accordingly
```

This example replaces a quadratic-time nested loop approach with a linear-time algorithm, greatly improving efficiency for large input sizes.

The table below defines key performance metrics formally:

Table 1.2: *Key Performance Metrics: Definitions and Formulas*

Metric	Definition and Formula
Response Time	Time interval between request initiation and completion. Measured as $T_{response} = T_{end} - T_{start}$
Throughput	Number of operations completed per unit time. Often calculated as Throughput $= \frac{\text{Total Operations}}{T_{total}}$
Latency	Delay before data transfer starts following an instruction. Similar to response time but often used for lower-level hardware or networking delays.
Resource Utilization	Percentage of time a resource is actively used. For example, CPU utilization $U_{CPU} = \frac{\text{CPU busy time}}{\text{Total elapsed time}} \times 100\%$
Bandwidth	Maximum data transfer rate of a system or network, typically measured in bits per second (bps).

For clarity and precision in optimization discussions, certain terms frequently arise. The notation $O(n)$ describes an algorithm whose running time grows linearly with input size n. Cache locality refers to the tendency of a program to access data stored close together in memory, enhancing cache efficiency and reducing latency. A program is termed I/O bound when its performance is limited primarily by input/output operations, such as disk reads or network communication.

11

Conversely, it is CPU bound if processor computation is the limiting factor instead. Understanding these terms helps contextualize performance issues and select appropriate optimizations.

The process of performance improvement is iterative and cyclical. It often follows a pattern of profiling to identify costly operations, analyzing data to locate bottlenecks, applying improvements, and retesting to verify progress. This cycle repeats until satisfactory performance levels are achieved or further gains become impractical.

```
repeat:
    profile_program()
    identify_bottlenecks()
    optimize_bottlenecks()
    test_performance()
until performance_goals_met or no_further_improvement
```

This disciplined workflow ensures continuous refinement based on measurable results rather than assumptions, enabling systematic and effective optimization.

By combining a solid understanding of terminology, trade-offs, measurement techniques, and strategic approaches, practitioners can navigate the complex landscape of performance optimization. Through iterative profiling and refinement, developers enhance software efficiency, responsiveness, and resource utilization, ultimately delivering higher quality applications tailored to practical constraints and user expectations.

1.3 Stages of Program Execution

The journey of a program from its conception as human-readable instructions to execution on a physical device encompasses several distinct stages. Understanding this lifecycle provides critical insight into where performance factors arise and how software interacts with the underlying hardware. This process begins with source code, passes through translation phases such as preprocessing, parsing, compilation, or interpretation, and culminates in execution by the central processing unit (CPU) and supporting hardware components.

Source code constitutes the initial input in the program execution pipeline. It consists of instructions written by developers in high-level programming languages designed to be human-readable and expressive. These instructions specify the behavior intended by the programmer, using syntax and constructs of languages such as C, Python, or Java. Source code abstracts away hardware details, allowing programmers to focus on logic and algorithms rather than machine-level operations.

Before the source code can be executed, it must undergo preparation known as preprocessing and parsing. Preprocessing involves simple text transformations, such as macro replacement or file inclusion, which are common in some languages like C and C++. Parsing is the syntactic analysis phase where the source code is examined to verify its adherence to the language grammar. During parsing, the compiler or interpreter breaks down the code into smaller units called tokens and organizes them into a structured representation, often an abstract syntax tree (AST). This representation serves as a foundation for subsequent translation or execution steps, ensuring the code's semantic

13

correctness and facilitating optimization.

Once parsing completes successfully, the code proceeds to one of two primary paths depending on the programming model in use: compilation or interpretation. Compilation involves transforming the high-level source code into a lower-level form, typically machine code or an intermediate representation. The compiler acts as a translator, converting language constructs into instructions understood directly by the processor or by a runtime environment. This process is usually done ahead of time, producing a separate executable file that can run independently. Compilers often perform various optimizations during translation to improve performance, such as eliminating redundant calculations or rearranging instructions to exploit hardware capabilities.

Interpretation, in contrast, executes the source code line-by-line or statement-by-statement at runtime without producing a standalone executable. The interpreter reads each instruction, analyzes it, and performs the specified operation immediately. This mode facilitates rapid development and testing since changes in code can be executed without recompilation. However, interpreted programs generally run more slowly than compiled ones because each instruction undergoes repeated parsing and decoding during execution.

Between these two extremes lies the use of intermediate code representations. Languages like Java and many modern frameworks use an intermediate form such as bytecode, which is compiled from source code but not directly executable by hardware. Instead, this intermediate code runs inside a virtual machine or runtime environment that interprets or further compiles the bytecode into machine instructions on the fly. This hybrid approach offers portability across hardware platforms while enabling optimizations through just-in-time (JIT) compilation techniques.

At the core of program execution is the hardware, mainly the CPU, which carries out the instructions produced by compilers or interpreters. The CPU operates by continuously fetching instructions from memory, decoding them to determine the operation required, and then executing the necessary computations or data manipulations. Memory hierarchy, including registers, caches, and main memory (RAM), supports the CPU by providing varying levels of fast storage to hold instructions and data. Efficient use of these memory layers significantly impacts execution speed, as access times differ greatly between registers, cache, and main memory.

The execution lifecycle of a program can be summarized with the following pseudocode illustrating the main stages:

```
1:  preprocess_source_code(source)
2:  parse_result = parse(preprocessed_source)
3:  if compiling:
4:      intermediate_code = compile(parse_result)
5:      executable = generate_executable(intermediate_code)
6:  else if interpreting:
7:      interpreter = initialize_interpreter(parse_result)
8:      while program_not_finished:
9:          instruction = interpreter.fetch_next_instruction()
10:         execute(instruction)
11: else if intermediate_execution:
12:     runtime_env = setup_runtime_environment(intermediate_code)
13:     runtime_env.execute()
```

The CPU's role is central during step 10 and step 13 where it performs the actual execution of instructions. Fetch-decode-execute cycles constitute the fundamental operation sequence. In each cycle, the CPU retrieves the next instruction address from the program counter, loads the instruction from memory, decodes it to identify the operation type and operands, executes the operation using arithmetic logic units (ALUs) or control units, and then updates the program counter to the next instruction. This cycle repeats at processor clock speeds that currently reach billions of cycles per second, determining how swiftly a program can run.

The efficiency of program execution also depends on memory subsystems that facilitate instruction and data access. The table below outlines the principal memory components commonly used during execution:

Table 1.3: *Memory Hierarchy in Program Execution*

Memory Type	Role and Characteristics
Registers	Small, fastest storage located within the CPU; hold data and instructions immediately needed for operations.
CPU Cache (L1, L2, L3)	Fast memory close to the CPU core used to minimize latency for frequently accessed data and instructions. Sizes vary from a few kilobytes to several megabytes.
Main Memory (RAM)	Larger, slower memory used to store programs and data during execution; accessible by CPU but with higher latency than caches.
Persistent Storage	Non-volatile memory such as hard drives or solid-state drives where programs and data reside when not actively executed; access times are orders of magnitude slower.

To illustrate the flow of program execution, the following simplified pseudocode shows how source code transitions through stages to run:

```
function execute_program(source_code):
    preprocessed = preprocess(source_code)
    parsed = parse(preprocessed)
    if requires_compilation:
        code = compile(parsed)
        load_into_memory(code)
    else if requires_interpretation:
        setup_interpreter(parsed)
    while not end_of_program:
        instruction = fetch_next_instruction()
        decode_and_execute(instruction)
```

This model reflects a common structure across many programming en-

16

vironments, although specific details vary with implementation strategies.

Optimization opportunities exist at every stage of this execution model. During compilation, compilers can perform static analysis and transformations to reduce code size, improve instruction scheduling, and exploit parallel hardware features. Preprocessing steps can simplify code and reduce unnecessary operations. Interpreters might use just-in-time compilation to translate frequently executed code paths dynamically into optimized machine code. On the hardware side, designing algorithms and data structures to maximize cache locality and minimize costly memory access improves throughput. Understanding the complete execution pipeline enables developers to apply targeted optimizations, reducing overhead and enhancing performance from source code to silicon.

Appreciating this comprehensive view of program execution helps bridge the gap between writing high-level code and achieving efficient runtime behavior. Each stage imposes constraints and possibilities for improvement, making the execution lifecycle an essential framework for performance-focused software engineering.

1.4 Performance Goals and Constraints

Setting realistic and well-defined performance goals is a foundational step in software development that significantly influences design choices, implementation strategies, and overall project success. These goals must arise from a careful analysis of project requirements, user expectations, and system limitations to ensure that performance targets are both meaningful and achievable within given constraints.

Understanding project requirements involves a thorough assessment of the software's intended use, scope, and user needs. This process includes identifying critical scenarios where performance directly impacts functionality or user satisfaction. For instance, an interactive application designed for real-time responsiveness demands low latency, whereas a data-processing backend might prioritize high throughput. Constraints such as target platforms, expected workload, and operational environment must also be analyzed to shape appropriate performance objectives. Recognizing these factors early guides the selection of relevant metrics and the scope of optimization efforts.

Defining performance metrics constitutes the next essential step. Performance can be quantified through various parameters depending on system characteristics and goals. Common metrics include response time, which measures delay between user action and system reaction; throughput, indicating the volume of operations or data processed per unit time; and resource consumption, encompassing CPU usage, memory footprint, network bandwidth, and energy usage. These metrics provide objective criteria to evaluate whether the software meets defined requirements and to monitor its behavior under different conditions.

Once metrics are established, setting realistic targets requires aligning desired outcomes with hardware capabilities, software environments, and user expectations. Benchmarks must account for the performance ranges typical on the intended platforms. For example, mobile devices with limited processing power and battery life impose stricter resource usage limits than high-performance servers. Additionally, user tolerance thresholds, such as acceptable delays in application response, influence target specification. Setting overambitious goals without considering such practical factors may lead to wasted effort or unrealistic

18

deadlines, while overly lenient targets risk delivering substandard experiences.

Performance goals often demand balancing trade-offs among competing priorities. Speed improvements might come at the cost of increased memory consumption, or reducing resource demands may complicate code structure and hinder maintainability. Decisions must reflect project priorities and contextual constraints. For example, a safety-critical system may emphasize reliability and predictability over maximal speed, while a consumer-facing application might favor responsiveness above all. Explicitly identifying these priorities guides design decisions and resource allocation, ensuring that optimization efforts address the most impactful areas.

Resource constraints impose additional limits on achievable performance. Hardware capacity, including processing power, available memory, and network bandwidth, determines physical boundaries that software must operate within. Budgetary restrictions may limit the ability to procure high-end hardware or extend development time. Deadlines and team expertise influence how deeply and extensively performance can be optimized. Acknowledging these constraints is vital to avoid pursuing targets that are infeasible or economically unjustifiable.

Documenting performance goals early and clearly is a best practice that fosters alignment among development teams, stakeholders, and users. Goals should be specific, measurable, attainable, relevant, and time-bound (SMART). Well-maintained documentation assists in tracking progress, facilitates communication, and provides a baseline for validation and regression testing throughout the development life cycle.

Establishing baseline measurements through benchmarking provides actionable data for comparison and improvement. The following sample code snippet illustrates how to measure the execution time of a function, a basic form of benchmarking:

```
import time

def benchmark_function(func, *args, **kwargs):
    start_time = time.perf_counter()
    result = func(*args, **kwargs)
    end_time = time.perf_counter()
    elapsed_time = end_time - start_time
    print(f"Execution time: {elapsed_time:.6f} seconds")
    return result

# Example usage
def example_task(n):
    total = 0
    for i in range(n):
        total += i
    return total

benchmark_function(example_task, 1000000)
```

This approach quantifies performance in controlled environments, enabling subsequent comparisons as modifications are applied.

Typical constraints encountered in performance goal setting appear in Table 1.4, illustrating the range and nature of restrictions to consider.

Performance goals are seldom static and may evolve throughout the development process. Changes in project scope, technological advancements, or emerging user feedback can necessitate revising targets. Flexibility in adjusting goals while maintaining focus on core priorities ensures that optimization remains aligned with real-world conditions and delivers sustained value.

To make informed decisions when balancing competing trade-offs, decision processes can be structured algorithmically. The following pseu-

Table 1.4: *Typical Performance Constraints*

Constraint Type	Description
Latency Limits	Maximum allowable delay for critical operations, e.g., user interface response under 100 milliseconds.
Throughput Requirements	Minimum operations per second, such as processing 1000 transactions per minute.
Memory Budget	Upper bounds on usable RAM to avoid system thrashing or crashes.
CPU Utilization	Limits on processor usage to prevent overheating or interference with other tasks.
Energy Consumption	Caps aimed at conserving battery life on mobile devices or reducing operational costs.
Network Bandwidth	Restrictions on data transfer rates due to infrastructure or cost considerations.
Development Time	Deadlines and resource availability that constrain optimization efforts.

docode outlines a simplified approach to select among optimization options based on priorities:

```
function select_optimization(options, priorities):
    best_option = null
    highest_score = -infinity
    for option in options:
        score = 0
        if priorities.speed:
            score += evaluate_speed_gain(option) * priorities.
    speed_weight
        if priorities.memory:
            score += evaluate_memory_usage(option) * priorities.
    memory_weight
        if priorities.energy:
            score += evaluate_energy_savings(option) * priorities.
    energy_weight
        # Add other criteria as needed
        if score > highest_score:
            highest_score = score
            best_option = option
    return best_option
```

Such systematic evaluation supports objective optimization planning, accounting for all relevant factors.

Continuous monitoring and iterative refinement play crucial roles in maintaining and achieving performance goals. Feedback from profiling, testing, and user analytics provides valuable information on the actual behavior of software in operational contexts. By regularly comparing measured metrics against documented targets, teams can identify deviations, diagnose causes, and implement corrective measures. This agile approach to performance management ensures quality is sustained and enhanced as the software evolves.

Establishing performance goals grounded in comprehensive understanding of project needs, realistic assessments, and strategic prioritization forms the basis for effective optimization. Through careful documentation, benchmarking, adaptive decision-making, and iterative improvement, development teams can deliver software that meets user expectations while operating efficiently within available resources.

1.5 Navigating This Book

To derive the greatest benefit from this text, it is advisable to approach the material in a carefully structured sequence, progressing from foundational concepts toward more advanced topics. The opening chapters establish essential terminology and principles that provide a solid base for understanding subsequent content. As the reader advances, chapters introduce deeper technical details and practical techniques to refine programming performance. Following the recommended reading order will facilitate cumulative learning, allowing each section to build upon knowledge gained earlier. While some sections can be explored independently, adhering to this sequence supports coherent comprehension and skill development.

Prior to engaging with the book's content, readers should possess a basic proficiency in programming concepts and practices. A fundamental understanding of variables, control structures such as loops and conditionals, functions or procedures, and simple data manipulation is necessary to grasp discussions on performance optimization. Familiarity with at least one programming language and the ability to write basic code will enable readers to interact meaningfully with examples and exercises. This background knowledge ensures that attention can focus on performance principles rather than introductory programming constructs.

Active reading strategies significantly enhance knowledge acquisition and retention. As the material presents new concepts and specialized terminology, taking thoughtful notes can clarify ideas and provide reference points for revision. Readers are encouraged to pause regularly to summarize what they have learned and formulate questions that deepen their engagement. Working through exercises and experimental coding examples embedded within chapters reinforces abstract theory through practical application. Setting aside dedicated time for reflection after each major topic allows for consolidation of understanding and identification of areas requiring further study.

The examples and exercises interspersed throughout this book serve a vital pedagogical function. They are designed not merely to illustrate principles but to foster hands-on skills essential for implementation. Engaging actively with example code—by typing it out, modifying parameters, and observing effects—provides experiential insight that complements textual explanations. Exercises challenge readers to apply concepts creatively and critically, building confidence and technical proficiency. Readers should approach these learning opportunities deliberately, using them to test comprehension and expand problem-solving abilities.

Supplementary learning resources can accelerate mastery and broaden perspectives. The table below compiles recommendations for external tutorials, software tools, and online communities supportive of performance optimization topics.

Table 1.5: *Additional Resources*

Resource Type	Description and Examples
Tutorials	Online courses on algorithms, data structures, and programming languages (e.g., Coursera, edX)
Software Tools	Profilers (e.g., Valgrind, VisualVM), debuggers, benchmarking libraries
Communities	Forums such as Stack Overflow, Reddit's programming subreddits, GitHub repositories for collaborative learning
Documentation	Official language manuals and API references to clarify syntax and library functions
Books	Complementary texts on algorithm design, software engineering, and system architecture

Periodic self-assessment is a useful technique to gauge progress and identify concepts requiring reinforcement. After completing chapters or topic clusters, readers should challenge themselves with quizzes, reattempt exercises, or attempt to explain key ideas in their own words. Reflecting on problem-solving approaches and results aids metacognition and directs future study efforts. Maintaining a record of achievements and difficulties can foster a growth mindset and enhance motivation throughout the learning journey.

To facilitate systematic progress tracking, readers may employ simple tools such as checklists or learning journals. The following code snippet illustrates a basic approach to logging topic completion and exercise performance in a structured text format:

```
class LearningTracker:
```

```
    def __init__(self):
        self.completed = {}

    def mark_complete(self, topic):
        self.completed[topic] = True
        print(f"Marked '{topic}' as completed.")

    def is_completed(self, topic):
        return self.completed.get(topic, False)

    def summary(self):
        print("Progress Summary:")
        for topic, done in self.completed.items():
            status = 'Done' if done else 'Pending'
            print(f"- {topic}: {status}")

# Example usage
tracker = LearningTracker()
tracker.mark_complete("Chapter 1: Introduction")
tracker.mark_complete("Chapter 2: Performance Metrics")
tracker.summary()
```

Documenting progress provides tangible evidence of achievement and assists in planning remaining study activities.

Maximizing practical application of learned principles amplifies the educational value of this book. Readers are encouraged to undertake small projects that incorporate performance optimization techniques, participate in coding bootcamps, or engage with real-world challenges on platforms such as coding competitions or open-source contributions. Applying concepts in varied contexts deepens understanding, reveals unforeseen complexities, and accelerates skill acquisition necessary for professional growth.

Collaboration and community involvement constitute powerful avenues to expand knowledge and resolve difficulties. Joining study groups, online forums, or local programming meetups exposes readers to diverse problem-solving perspectives and expert feedback. Engaging in peer discussions and mentorship relationships enhances critical thinking and exposes learners to best practices. Collaborative efforts often motivate sustained learning and provide support during challenging phases of mastering complex material.

Seeking constructive feedback from instructors, peers, or experienced mentors greatly benefits comprehension and skill refinement. Feedback helps identify misunderstandings, improve coding style, and optimize solutions more efficiently. It also encourages reflection on alternative approaches and clarifies subtle details that textual material alone may not fully convey. Readers should proactively request critiques and incorporate suggestions thoughtfully to continually elevate their competency.

By following the guidance presented here—progressing through the material deliberately, leveraging active learning tactics, utilizing supplementary resources, and engaging collaboratively—readers will position themselves to extract maximum value from this book and develop robust expertise in performance optimization. The structured learning path, combined with intentional practice and reflection, paves the way for transformative growth in both knowledge and applied skill.

2

Understanding Program Performance

This chapter defines key performance metrics such as execution time, through-put, latency, and resource usage, explaining their relevance to evaluating soft-ware efficiency. It explores how computers execute code, including the roles of interpreters, compilers, and hardware components like CPUs. Factors influencing performance, such as algorithm choice, data handling, and input size, are examined in detail. Common pitfalls that degrade performance, like inefficient loops and memory misuse, are highlighted to help avoid these issues. The chapter also discusses methods for measuring and monitoring performance to facilitate continuous improvement.

2.1 Defining Program Performance and Key Metrics

In evaluating the efficiency of a program, several core metrics are essential for understanding how well the software performs in practice. These metrics provide quantitative measures that describe different facets of program execution, allowing developers to identify bottlenecks, optimize resource usage, and improve overall system responsiveness. The most fundamental metrics include *execution time, throughput, latency*, and *resource usage*. Each metric captures a distinct aspect of performance, and together they offer a comprehensive view of a program's operational characteristics.

Execution Time refers to the total duration a program or a specific operation takes from start to finish. It is one of the most direct indicators of speed and often the first attribute examined when performance is considered. For example, when a function is called, the time taken until it completes is its execution time. This measurement includes all processing delays, including CPU cycles consumed, memory accesses, and any other system interactions involved in completing the task. Execution time is measured in units such as seconds, milliseconds, or microseconds depending on the granularity required. Reducing the execution time of critical code sections directly improves user-perceived responsiveness and system throughput.

Throughput measures the amount of work or data a system can process in a given unit of time. Unlike execution time, which focuses on the duration of a single task, throughput evaluates the system's capacity to handle multiple tasks or data volume over time. For example, in a web server context, throughput might be measured as the number of HTTP requests processed per second. High throughput implies efficient handling of workloads and is especially relevant in systems with concurrent or repetitive operations. Maximizing throughput is vital for applications such as database servers, batch processing systems, and network data pipelines, where volume-oriented performance is paramount.

Latency represents the delay between the initiation of a request or input and the start of the corresponding processing or response. It is frequently associated with system responsiveness and is critical in real-time applications where delays must be minimized to maintain usability. For instance, in interactive software or online video games, low latency ensures that user actions are reflected almost instantaneously in the system output. Latency differs from execution time in that it focuses on the delay before an operation begins or a response is initiated, while execution time covers the entire duration of the operation. Understanding and minimizing latency is crucial in user-facing systems, embedded devices, and communication protocols.

Resource Usage quantifies how much of the system's computational resources are consumed during program execution. This includes CPU cycles, memory (RAM), disk or storage input/output activity, and network bandwidth utilization. Monitoring resource usage helps in identifying inefficiencies and potential bottlenecks that limit performance. For example, excessive memory usage may indicate memory leaks or unnecessary data retention, leading to degraded performance or system instability. Similarly, high CPU utilization might reflect inefficient algorithms or busy-wait loops. Disk I/O and network consumption are important in applications involving large datasets or substantial communication, where such resources often become limiting factors. Efficient resource management ensures that the program runs

29

smoothly without overloading the system or causing contention with other processes.

Metric	Formula
Response Time	$R = S + W$, where S is service time and W is waiting time
Throughput	$X = \frac{N}{T}$, where N is the number of completed tasks and T is the total time
CPU Utilization	$U = \frac{\text{CPU Busy Time}}{\text{Total Observation Time}} \times 100\%$
Latency	Time delay between request and start of processing

Table 2.1: *Key Performance Metrics and Their Formulas*

To illustrate these concepts, consider a simple example of measuring execution time in Python. By recording the time before and after a block of code executes, one can determine its duration precisely:

```python
import time

start_time = time.time()
# Code block to measure
for i in range(1000000):
    pass
end_time = time.time()

execution_time = end_time - start_time
print(f"Execution Time: {execution_time} seconds")
```

```
Execution Time: 0.034567 seconds
```

This approach provides direct insight into the duration of a specific computation, which is valuable for performance evaluation and tuning.

While the definitions of these metrics are straightforward, their relationship often involves trade-offs. Increasing throughput, for example, might cause a rise in latency if tasks queue up while waiting for processing. Similarly, aggressively reducing execution time by utilizing more CPU resources can increase resource usage to unsustainable levels, affecting overall system stability. Balancing these metrics requires an understanding of the application's context and requirements—whether prioritizing low latency for responsiveness or high throughput for volume processing.

Real-world scenarios further highlight the importance of these metrics. For example, a video streaming service must maintain low latency to prevent buffering delays during playback, while achieving high throughput to serve many users simultaneously. In contrast, scientific computation programs often focus on minimizing execution time of complex calculations to boost productivity. Embedded systems, especially those controlling industrial machinery, must carefully balance resource usage against stringent hardware constraints.

Execution time quantifies how fast a program completes tasks, throughput measures the volume of work processed over time, latency describes the delay before processing begins, and resource usage assesses the consumption of system components. Mastery of these metrics enables developers to evaluate software performance effectively and make informed optimization decisions tailored to specific operational goals.

2.2 How Computers Execute Code

At the core of software development lies the process through which human-written instructions are transformed into executable actions performed by a computer's hardware. This transformation encompasses multiple layers, starting from writing source code in a high-level programming language to the final execution of machine instructions by the central processing unit (CPU). Understanding this flow clarifies the roles of compilers, interpreters, and the CPU, and provides insight into key performance considerations.

The initial step involves *writing source code*, where developers express algorithms and logic using human-readable programming languages such as Python, Java, or C++. These languages provide abstractions and syntax designed to be understandable by humans, facilitating the communication of computational tasks without requiring direct knowledge of hardware details. Source code consists of statements, expressions, and declarations structured according to the language's grammar, intended to describe what the program should do.

Once written, the source code undergoes *parsing and lexical analysis*, crucial processes in translating high-level code into forms that machines can understand. Lexical analysis, or tokenization, breaks the raw code into fundamental units called tokens—these include keywords, operators, identifiers, and literals. Parsing then interprets these tokens according to the language's grammar rules, constructing a syntactic structure known as the parse tree or abstract syntax tree (AST). This structured representation captures the logical composition and relationships of code elements, enabling further processing by compilers or interpreters.

Following analysis, the code is transformed in one of two primary ways: by compilation or by interpretation. The *compilation process* translates the entire high-level source code into machine code—binary instructions directly executable by the CPU—before the program runs. This translation is typically performed by a compiler, which converts source code into either native machine instructions or an intermediate representation that can later be optimized and converted. For example, C++ programs are usually compiled ahead of time into machine code tailored for the target hardware. Compilation often includes optimization steps that improve performance by rearranging code, eliminating redundancies, and applying hardware-specific improvements.

In contrast, the *interpretation process* involves executing source code line-by-line or statement-by-statement at runtime without producing a separate machine code file beforehand. An interpreter reads, parses, and directly simulates the instructions, performing operations immediately as it encounters them. Languages like Python and JavaScript frequently use interpretation to provide flexibility and ease of development. Although this results in slower execution compared to compiled code—because interpretation adds overhead for parsing and dispatching at runtime—it offers benefits such as easier debugging and platform independence.

Many programming environments use *intermediate code* as a compromise between compilation and interpretation. Intermediate code, such as bytecode, is a platform-independent, low-level representation of the source program. Bytecode is not directly executable by hardware but is interpreted or further compiled by a virtual machine (VM) or runtime environment tailored to the target platform. Java's Virtual Machine (JVM) and the Common Language Runtime (CLR) for .NET languages use bytecode to achieve portability and enable runtime optimizations. This layered approach combines the speed advantages of compiled code with the flexibility of interpretation.

Central to understanding execution is the *role of the CPU*, the hardware component that physically performs computations and controls program flow. The CPU processes instructions by fetching them from memory, decoding the instructions to determine the required operation, and executing them sequentially or out-of-order for performance. This fundamental cycle—known as the *fetch-decode-execute*

33

cycle—repeats continuously during program execution, driving the behavior encoded in the software.

The simplified pseudocode below illustrates this cycle:

```
while (true) {
    instruction = fetch_from_memory(PC)
    decoded_op = decode_instruction(instruction)
    execute(decoded_op)
    PC = PC + instruction_length
}
```

Here, the program counter (PC) points to the address of the next instruction to fetch. The CPU retrieves the instruction, decodes its meaning, performs the specified operation (such as arithmetic, memory access, or branching), and advances the PC to the subsequent instruction. This cycle is repeated rapidly, often billions of times per second in modern processors.

The efficiency of this cycle is influenced by the *memory hierarchy*, which includes various levels of storage with differing speeds and capacities. The CPU accesses data and instructions through multiple layers: several levels of cache memory (L1, L2, L3), main memory (RAM), and persistent storage such as solid-state drives (SSD) or hard disk drives (HDD). Access to cache memory is orders of magnitude faster than RAM or disk, and effective use of caching significantly affects execution performance.

Programs that maximize cache locality—ensuring data needed soon is loaded into fast cache memory—can execute significantly faster due to reduced memory latency. Operations requiring frequent disk access suffer delays because persistent storage is much slower.

The *compiler/interpreter role* differs in how they prepare code for exe-

Memory Level	Access Time (ns)	Typical Size	Purpose
L1 Cache	0.5–1	16–64 KB	Immediate CPU access for instructions and data
L2 Cache	3–10	256 KB–1 MB	Larger but slower cache
L3 Cache	10–30	Several MB	Shared cache across CPU cores
RAM	50–100	GB range	Main system memory
Disk Storage	10,000,000+	TB range	Persistent data storage

Table 2.2: *Memory Hierarchy and Typical Access Times*

cution. Compilers convert entire programs ahead of time to machine code, which the CPU can run directly. This allows extensive optimizations but requires recompilation for each target platform. Interpreters execute code on-the-fly, providing ease of development and portability at the expense of raw speed. Many modern runtime environments combine both, using Just-In-Time (JIT) compilation to translate intermediate code into machine code dynamically during execution, blending speed and flexibility.

Runtime code optimization techniques like JIT compilers analyze frequently executed code sections and optimize them while the program runs, tailoring instructions to the actual workload and hardware. This dynamic optimization can improve performance beyond what static compilation achieves, especially in long-running applications.

The process of translating human-readable source code into executable actions involves multiple stages: source code writing, lexical and syntactic analysis, compilation or interpretation to produce executable or intermediate code, and finally, instruction execution by the CPU through repeated fetch-decode-execute cycles. Awareness of these layers and their interaction aids developers in understanding performance characteristics and optimization opportunities during software development.

2.3   Factors Affecting Performance

The performance of a program depends on a complex interplay of various factors that influence how efficiently it executes and utilizes resources. These factors range from the choice of algorithms and data handling techniques to the characteristics of underlying hardware and the size and complexity of input data. Understanding these influences is essential for optimizing software and making informed development decisions.

At the foundation lies *algorithm choice*, which has a profound effect on both execution time and resource consumption. Algorithms define the specific steps and procedures a program follows to solve a problem, and their efficiency is often expressed in terms of time and space complexity. For example, searching for an element in an unsorted list using a linear search algorithm requires inspecting each item until a match is found, taking time proportional to the size of the list (linear time). In contrast, a binary search algorithm applied to a sorted list reduces the number of necessary comparisons dramatically, completing in logarithmic time. Choosing an efficient algorithm minimizes computation, reduces unnecessary operations, and often significantly accelerates program execution.

Closely related to algorithms is the way data is handled during execution. *Data handling techniques* encompass the selection and use of data structures, the organization of data in memory, and access patterns. Data structures such as arrays, linked lists, hash tables, and trees each provide different trade-offs in terms of insertion, deletion, and lookup speed. For instance, arrays offer constant-time access by index but costly insertions, while linked lists excel in dynamic insertion but lack direct indexing. Moreover, memory locality—the arrangement of data to maximize usage of the CPU cache—strongly impacts speed. When data is stored and accessed sequentially, it leverages spatial locality, allowing the CPU to fetch data efficiently in blocks. Irregular or sparse data access patterns lead to cache misses, forcing slower memory accesses and degrading performance.

The physical *hardware characteristics* on which a program runs also shape its performance constraints and opportunities. Modern CPUs vary in architecture, number of cores, clock speed, and cache hierarchy. Larger and faster caches improve data availability to the processor and reduce reliance on slower main memory. Memory bandwidth determines how quickly data can be transferred between CPU and RAM, while storage types (SSD vs. HDD) affect read/write speeds for file operations. Applications designed with awareness of these hardware traits can tailor their execution to exploit characteristics such as multi-core parallelism or cache-friendly data layouts, thereby improving speed and responsiveness.

An additional critical factor is the *input size and scale*. As input data grows larger or more complex, computational workload correspondingly increases. An efficient algorithm that performs well on small datasets may become impractical at large scales if its time complexity grows rapidly. For example, an algorithm with quadratic time complexity (proportional to the square of input size) may be acceptable with inputs of a thousand items but become infeasible for millions of items. Understanding how execution time scales with input size guides algorithm selection and system design to maintain performance as data expands.

Exploiting *parallelism and concurrency* offers substantial performance gains by utilizing multiple CPU cores or threads to execute computations simultaneously. Parallelism involves dividing a task into independent subtasks running in parallel, while concurrency manages multiple tasks in overlapping time periods, possibly interacting or sharing resources. Programs that are designed to be parallelizable can reduce total execution time for suitable problems, such as large-scale numerical computations or processing numerous independent requests. However, concurrency adds complexity due to synchronization and potential contention for shared resources.

Compiler and runtime environments also influence performance through *compiler and runtime optimizations*. Modern compilers provide options or flags to enable aggressive optimizations that improve code execution speed, reduce size, or enhance resource usage. These optimizations include inlining functions, loop unrolling, dead code elimination, and vectorization, among others. At runtime, virtual machines or interpreters may apply dynamic optimizations such as Just-In-Time (JIT) compilation, which translates and optimizes code segments during execution based on actual usage patterns, further enhancing efficiency.

However, *resource contention* can limit the benefits of these improvements. When multiple processes or threads compete for shared CPUs, memory bandwidth, or I/O channels, bottlenecks arise, reducing overall throughput. For example, excessive threading without regard for hardware limits can lead to context switching overhead and cache thrashing. Similarly, simultaneous access to disk or network resources may cause delays, negating gains in pure computation speed. Effective performance optimization must therefore consider the potential for contention and design software to minimize conflicting demands.

Profiling tools play a crucial role in identifying performance bottlenecks and guiding optimization efforts. The following snippet demonstrates usage of Python's built-in cProfile module to profile a function's runtime behavior:

```
import cProfile

def compute():
    total = 0
    for i in range(100000):
        total += i ** 2
    return total

cProfile.run('compute()')
```

This profiling output indicates how much time is spent in each function call, enabling developers to focus their efforts on the most costly operations.

The impact of hardware choices on application performance is significant and can be summarized by comparing various configurations as in Table 2.3. This table illustrates typical effects of CPU speed, number of cores, RAM size, and storage type on diverse performance metrics:

Hardware Aspect	CPU Speed	Cores	RAM Size	Storage Type
Execution Speed	High	Moderate	Moderate	Low
Parallel Throughput	Moderate	High	Moderate	Low
Memory Capacity	Low	Low	High	–
I/O Bandwidth	Low	Low	Moderate	High
Cost	High	High	Moderate	Variable

Table 2.3: *Impact of Hardware Configurations on Performance*

As input size expands, the growth of execution time can be modeled and visualized to anticipate performance degradation. The pseudocode below describes a typical scaling behavior for an algorithm

39

with quadratic time complexity:

```
function process(input):
    for i = 1 to length(input):
        for j = 1 to length(input):
            perform_operation(input[i], input[j])
```

Here, the number of operations grows proportionally to the square of the input size, meaning execution time increases rapidly as input grows. Identifying such scaling behaviors enables developers to choose or design more efficient solutions before encountering severe performance issues.

Overall, program performance cannot be fully understood without considering the combined effects of algorithmic design, data management, hardware capabilities, input characteristics, and system-level factors such as concurrency and resource contention. Profiling and benchmarking tools assist in pinpointing performance challenges, guiding developers toward targeted improvements that leverage both software and hardware strengths.

2.4   Common Performance Pitfalls

Performance optimization requires careful attention to how code is written and executed. Many software inefficiencies arise from widespread and often avoidable mistakes. Recognizing these common pitfalls early can significantly improve execution speed, reduce resource consumption, and enhance system responsiveness. Some of the universal performance issues include inefficient loop constructs, memory misuse, suboptimal input/output operations, and poor algorithm choices.

Loops constitute a fundamental part of programming, but *inefficient loop constructs* are among the most frequent sources of performance degradation. Redundant iterations or unnecessary repeated calculations within loops increase execution time without adding value. For instance, recalculating values inside a nested loop that remain constant during the iteration wastes CPU cycles. Additionally, looping over data structures inefficiently—such as using nested loops when a hash-based lookup would suffice—can result in exponential slowdowns. Writing concise loops that minimize work and avoid redundant operations is essential for scalable performance.

Memory misuse also negatively impacts program efficiency. This includes memory leaks where resources allocated dynamically are not released, causing gradual consumption of memory leading to sluggishness or system crashes. Fragmentation occurs when allocated memory becomes scattered, reducing access speed and increasing overhead for allocation and deallocation. Excessive or unnecessary memory allocations within frequently called functions introduce overhead that interrupts execution flow. Managing memory allocation carefully, using appropriate data types, and employing techniques like object pooling can mitigate these issues and maintain smooth operation.

Input/output (I/O) operations, such as reading from or writing to disk or network, are inherently slower than CPU or memory operations. *Suboptimal I/O* practices, like performing many small, unbatched reads or writes, significantly limit throughput. Each I/O call may involve system context switches and physical device latency, which accumulates when operations are uncoordinated. Grouping data and batching I/O reduces the frequency of costly operations, improving overall performance. Additionally, asynchronous I/O can prevent blocking the CPU during long waits.

Choosing inefficient algorithms contributes heavily to performance problems, especially as data scales. *Ignoring algorithm complexity* means using approaches with high time or space complexity without regard for input size. Algorithms with quadratic or cubic complexity that work acceptably on small datasets can cause insurmountable delays when applied to larger inputs. Profiling and understanding theoretical complexities help avoid these pitfalls by enabling developers to select or design better algorithms suitable for expected workloads.

Another subtle but detrimental issue is *unnecessary data copying*. Copying large data structures repeatedly—such as arrays, lists, or strings—without need creates overhead that prolongs runtime and increases memory usage. Immutable data structures or passing references instead of entire objects wherever possible can reduce copying costs, conserving time and memory.

Efficient use of the CPU's cache is critical for performance, yet many programs demonstrate a *lack of caching optimization*. When data accesses are random or poorly localized, caches suffer frequent misses forcing the CPU to fetch data from slower memory tiers. Structuring data and algorithms to maximize spatial and temporal locality—accessing contiguous blocks and reusing recent data—leverages the memory hierarchy to accelerate processing.

Long-running blocking operations pose another serious hindrance. Both *blocking input/output* and synchronization constructs like locks can cause CPUs to idle unnecessarily. When a thread waits for I/O completion or is blocked acquiring a resource, the processor cycles are wasted that could be utilized by other ready tasks. Employing non-blocking or asynchronous approaches alongside fine-grained locking strategies helps maintain high CPU utilization.

Code duplication indirectly harms performance and maintainability. Repeated code blocks introduce the risk of inconsistent updates and prevent effective reuse. While duplicated code may appear harmless, it hampers optimization opportunities such as inlining or better compiler analysis. Refactoring to eliminate duplication results in clearer, more efficient programs.

Using *non-optimized data structures* is another frequent misstep. For example, employing a linked list where fast access by index is critical leads to slow lookups, while using arrays in scenarios requiring frequent insertions or deletions causes extensive copying. Matching data structures to access patterns and algorithm requirements is essential to achieve expected performance levels.

Table 2.4 summarizes common pitfalls with their causes and recommended remedies:

Performance Pitfall	Root Cause	Recommended Remedy
Inefficient loops	Redundant calculations and excessive iterations	Move invariant computations outside loops, reduce nested loops, use efficient data accesses
Memory misuse	Leaks, fragmentation, excessive allocation	Use proper cleanup, memory pooling, prefer stack allocation where possible
Suboptimal I/O	Frequent small I/O calls, blocking operations	Batch I/O, use asynchronous methods, buffer data
Ignoring algorithm complexity	Using high-complexity algorithms on large data	Analyze complexity, choose or design efficient algorithms
Unnecessary data copying	Copying large objects unnecessarily	Pass references, use immutable structures carefully, minimize copies
Lack of cache optimization	Poor memory locality and random data access	Arrange data in contiguous regions, optimize loop ordering
Blocking operations	Synchronous I/O or locks causing idling	Use non-blocking I/O, fine-grained locks, or lock-free data structures
Code duplication	Repeated code fragments	Refactor for reuse and modularity
Non-optimized data structures	Unsuitable structures for task requirements	Choose data structures matching access and modification patterns

Table 2.4: *Common Performance Pitfalls: Causes and Remedies*

One frequent example of inefficient looping is shown in the Python snippet below, where a nested loop contains a computation repeated unnecessarily inside the inner loop:

```python
# Inefficient version
for i in range(len(data)):
    for j in range(len(data)):
        result = expensive_function(data[i], data[j] * 2)

# Optimized version
for i in range(len(data)):
    for j in range(len(data)):
        val = data[j] * 2  # Compute outside expensive_function
```

```
result = expensive_function(data[i], val)
```

By moving the multiplication data[j] * 2 outside the function call, the program avoids recomputing it each time as part of the inner loop body, reducing redundant calculation and improving speed.

The broader process of identifying and addressing performance pitfalls can be outlined in the following pseudocode:

```
function optimize_program(code):
    profile_results = profile(code)
    bottlenecks = identify_slowest_sections(profile_results)

    for section in bottlenecks:
        if section.contains_inefficient_loops():
            refactor_loops(section)
        if section.has_memory_issues():
            fix_memory_management(section)
        if section.has_suboptimal_io():
            batch_io_operations(section)
        if section.uses_bad_algorithms():
            replace_algorithms(section)
        if section.data_copying_unnecessary():
            minimize_data_copy(section)
        if section.lacks_cache_locality():
            improve_data_layout(section)
        if section.has_blocking_calls():
            implement_non_blocking(section)
    reprofile_and_repeat()
```

This iterative approach, combining profiling, targeted remediation, and validation, is instrumental in systematically improving software performance and avoiding common pitfalls that degrade efficiency.

By understanding and addressing these prevalent issues, developers can produce faster, more responsive software that scales effectively under growing workloads while conserving system resources.

2.5   Evaluating and Tracking Performance

Accurate evaluation and continuous tracking of a program's performance are essential to ensure software meets required efficiency goals
and sustains improvements over time. Performance measurement involves a combination of approaches—benchmarking, profiling, and
monitoring—that collectively provide a detailed understanding of how
the software behaves under various conditions. Implementing systematic measurement and tracking enables developers to detect regressions promptly, identify bottlenecks for optimization, and validate the
impact of changes.

Benchmarking constitutes a controlled and reproducible method for
assessing the performance of specific code sections or entire programs. Benchmarks are standardized tests designed to simulate typical workloads or critical operations, executed repeatedly under consistent conditions to obtain reliable timing or resource utilization metrics.
Through benchmarking, developers establish baselines for comparison
across versions, configurations, or algorithms. Benchmarks should be
designed to isolate aspects of interest and minimize external interference such as background processes or hardware variability.

A simple benchmarking example in Python uses the `timeit` module to
measure the average execution time of a function:

```
import timeit

def compute():
    total = 0
    for i in range(1000000):
        total += i*i
    return total

# Run the benchmark 10 times and take the average
```

```
execution_time = timeit.timeit(compute, number=10) / 10
print(f"Average execution time: {execution_time:.5f} seconds")
```

This code snippet runs the compute function ten times and calculates the average duration, yielding a stable measurement useful for comparing optimizations or alternative implementations.

Beyond benchmarking, *profiling tools* offer deeper insight by identifying which parts of the code consume the most execution time or resources. Profilers instrument the program or analyze runtime behavior to generate detailed call graphs, function-level timings, and invocation counts. Common and widely used profilers include gprof (for C and C++), VisualVM (for Java applications), and perf (a Linux profiling utility). These tools differ in capabilities but typically support sampling or instrumentation modes, enabling developers to pinpoint hotspots and inefficient code paths for focused optimization.

During execution, systems can be equipped to *monitor runtime metrics* such as CPU utilization, memory consumption, disk I/O, and network activity. Monitoring tools collect these metrics continuously or at intervals, providing visibility into the program's resource demands and identifying abnormal behaviors or resource exhaustion. Integrating system-level monitoring with application logging helps correlate performance characteristics with specific workload patterns or events, facilitating root cause identification.

Incorporating *automated testing for performance* expands quality assurance by detecting regressions introduced in new code commits or releases. Automated performance regression tests execute predefined benchmarks or scenarios as part of continuous integration pipelines, comparing current metrics against historical baselines. Alerts triggered by significant deviations notify developers early, preventing per-

47

formance degradation from reaching production. Automation ensures consistent evaluation and reduces manual testing effort.

Many frameworks and tools specialize in *performance tracking*, providing dashboards, trend analysis, and alerting mechanisms. Table 2.5 summarizes some popular solutions and their core features:

Tool	Type	Key Features	Typical Usage
Prometheus	Monitoring	Metrics collection, alerting, time-series data	Real-time system and application monitoring
Grafana	Visualization	Dashboard creation, data visualization from multiple sources	Performance trends and reporting
New Relic	APM	Application monitoring, tracing, error detection	Cloud and web application performance
JMH (Java)	Benchmarking	Microbenchmarking harness, JVM-specific tuning	Java method-level benchmarks
Google Benchmark	Benchmarking	Microbenchmarks, detailed statistical output	C++ code benchmarking

Table 2.5: *Sample Performance Tracking Tools and Frameworks*

Collecting and *storing performance data* systematically enables historical analysis and supports decision-making over longer periods. Efficient storage strategies involve time-series databases or structured log files indexed by timestamps and metadata such as configuration, environment, or workload type. Retaining sufficiently long history permits identification of trends, gradual degradations, or improvements linked to code changes or infrastructure modifications.

Visualizing performance metrics through charts and graphs facilitates understanding and communication with stakeholders. Common visualizations include line charts showing execution time variation across releases, bar graphs comparing resource usage among components, or heat maps indicating hotspots in code or system behavior. Automated generation of such visual reports integrated with monitoring systems accelerates detection of anomalies and illustrates progress of optimization efforts effectively.

```
Example Performance Metrics Visualization: Execution Time Over Multiple Runs

Run 1: |                     | 3.4s
Run 2: |                     | 4.1s
Run 3: |                     |
  6.0s
Run 4: |                     | 4.2s
Run 5: |                     | 5.0s
```

A critical element of performance tracking infrastructure is the capability to generate *automated alerts and reporting*. Alerts can be configured to trigger when metrics deviate from defined thresholds, such as execution time exceeding target limits or CPU utilization spiking unexpectedly. Reports summarizing performance statistics periodically assist teams in reviewing and planning further optimizations systematically.

All these measurement and tracking practices fit into an *iterative improvement cycle*: continuously measuring current behavior, analyzing collected data to find bottlenecks, implementing optimizations based on insights, and then re-measuring to verify gains. The cycle ensures ongoing refinement rather than one-time tuning, adapting software performance to evolving requirements and environments.

This process can be expressed in the following pseudocode:

```
while (software_in_development):
    metrics = measure_performance()
    analysis = analyze_metrics(metrics)
    optimizations = plan_improvements(analysis)
```

49

```
apply_optimizations(optimizations)
verify = remeasure_performance()
if verify indicates regression:
    rollback_changes()
```

Effective performance monitoring relies on *best practices* including integrating measurement tools early in development, automating data collection and testing, defining meaningful and actionable metrics, and involving multidisciplinary teams. Setting realistic performance targets aligned with user expectations and system constraints guides prioritization. Maintaining historical data and continuous dashboards enables proactive detection of issues before they impact users significantly.

Rigorous evaluation and tracking of program performance using benchmarking, profiling, monitoring, and automated testing form the backbone of a robust optimization strategy. These measures provide visibility into execution behavior, guide improvement efforts based on empirical data, and support sustained delivery of efficient software over time.

3

Efficient Data Structures

This chapter explains the importance of selecting appropriate data structures to enhance performance and efficiency. It covers fundamental structures such as arrays and lists, discussing their speed and memory trade-offs. The role of hash tables and maps in enabling fast lookups is examined, along with their use cases. Additionally, it explores trees and hierarchical data for efficient search and insertion operations. The chapter concludes with best practices and common pitfalls to avoid when choosing and implementing data structures for optimal performance.

3.1 The Role of Data Structures in Performance

Choosing the appropriate data structures is fundamental to developing efficient software. Data structures directly determine how data is stored, accessed, and manipulated, which in turn influences the overall speed and resource consumption of the program. Selecting an unsuit-

51

able data structure can impose unnecessary computational overhead, increasing execution time and memory usage, while a well-suited data structure optimizes these factors to enhance performance.

One of the primary considerations when selecting a data structure is its impact on time complexity, the measure of how the time required for operations grows as the amount of data increases. Different data structures support operations such as insertion, deletion, searching, and accessing data with varying efficiency. For example, accessing an element by index in an array typically executes in constant time, denoted as $O(1)$, whereas searching for an element in an unsorted linked list requires linear time, $O(n)$. Consequently, algorithms built upon inefficient data structures may experience performance degradation as input sizes scale, making the choice of structure critical for maintaining efficiency.

Memory usage considerations also play a vital role. Each data structure varies in its memory footprint depending on its internal organization and the overhead required for metadata. For instance, linked lists allocate additional memory for pointers linking elements, which increases overall consumption compared to arrays that store data contiguously. Excessive memory consumption can lead to increased paging, reduced cache effectiveness, and slower program execution. Thus, understanding the memory implications of a data structure enables programmers to optimize for constraints, especially in environments with limited resources.

Access and search speed differ among data structures due to how data is organized. Linear structures like arrays and lists require sequential traversal for certain operations, resulting in slower access times for large datasets. Conversely, data structures such as hash tables provide near constant time $O(1)$ average complexity for search, insertion, and deletion by computing a hash function that directly maps keys to memory locations. This capability allows rapid data retrieval, making hash tables highly suitable for scenarios demanding fast lookups. Understanding these characteristics facilitates selecting a structure aligned with performance requirements.

Insertion and deletion efficiency is similarly influenced by data structure design. Arrays, for example, require shifting elements to maintain order during insertions and deletions, which incurs linear time overhead $O(n)$ for these operations. In contrast, linked lists permit efficient insertions and deletions at arbitrary positions by adjusting pointers, often executing in constant time $O(1)$ if the node reference is known. Balanced tree structures maintain ordered data while providing logarithmic time $O(\log n)$ insertions and deletions, making them suitable for applications requiring sorted data with efficient updates. Selecting a data structure that aligns with expected mutation patterns can significantly improve performance.

Another often overlooked factor affecting performance is data locality and cache behavior. Modern computer architectures rely heavily on various levels of CPU caches to reduce memory access latency. Data structures that store elements contiguously in memory, such as arrays, benefit from spatial locality, whereby accessing one element brings neighboring elements into the cache, accelerating subsequent accesses. Conversely, pointer-based structures like linked lists tend to scatter elements throughout memory, reducing cache hit rates and increasing access latency. Optimizing data structures to enhance data locality can therefore yield tangible performance improvements by better utilizing processor caches.

The table below summarizes typical performance characteristics of several common data structures with respect to access, search, insertion, deletion, and memory usage:

Data Structure	Access	Search	Insertion	Deletion	Memory Usage
Array	$O(1)$	$O(n)$	$O(n)$	$O(n)$	Low
Linked List	$O(n)$	$O(n)$	$O(1)$	$O(1)$	Moderate
Hash Table	N/A	$O(1)$ avg	$O(1)$ avg	$O(1)$ avg	High
Binary Search Tree	$O(\log n)$ avg	$O(\log n)$ avg	$O(\log n)$ avg	$O(\log n)$ avg	Moderate
Balanced Tree (e.g., AVL)	$O(\log n)$	$O(\log n)$	$O(\log n)$	$O(\log n)$	Moderate

Table 3.1: *Performance characteristics of common data structures*

Choosing the right data structure necessitates balancing these performance aspects against the specific requirements of the application. Consider the example of a caching system that frequently retrieves stored values based on unique keys. A hash table is an obvious choice to optimize lookup speed, despite the higher memory overhead, because it provides near-instantaneous access. Conversely, if an application must maintain a sorted collection of elements supporting frequent insertions and deletions, a balanced binary search tree may offer the best trade-off between efficient updates and ordered traversal.

```cpp
#include <iostream>
#include <unordered_map>
#include <list>

// Suppose we want to track frequencies of words and preserve insertion
    order
int main() {
    std::list<std::string> insertion_order; // maintains order
    std::unordered_map<std::string, int> frequency_map; // fast lookup

    insertion_order.push_back("apple");
    frequency_map["apple"] = 1;

    insertion_order.push_back("banana");
```

```
frequency_map["banana"] = 2;

// Access frequency quickly
std::string key = "apple";
if (frequency_map.find(key) != frequency_map.end()) {
    std::cout << key << " appears " << frequency_map[key] << " times
.\n";
}

return 0;
}
```

This example demonstrates combining multiple data structures to optimize for different performance requirements: using an unordered map (hash table) for fast searches and a list to preserve insertion order, showcasing the necessity to choose structures based on the intended use case.

It is important to recognize that optimizing for one performance aspect often involves trade-offs in other areas. For instance, using a hash table to speed up lookups can increase memory usage, given the additional space required for hash buckets and handling collisions. Likewise, linked lists allow quick insertions but suffer from poor cache performance and slower data traversal due to pointer chasing. Thus, developers must carefully evaluate their priorities and constraints, as no single data structure universally optimizes all performance metrics.

The efficiency of algorithms depends heavily on the underlying data structures. An algorithm that searches for a value in a large dataset will perform drastically faster if the data is stored in a hash table or binary search tree compared to an unsorted list. Similarly, algorithms requiring frequent insertions must consider data structures with efficient update operations to avoid expensive reorganization costs. Designing algorithms without regard for data structure characteristics can result in suboptimal software that fails to scale.

To select data structures effectively, it is advisable to analyze the problem requirements, including the expected data size, operation types and frequencies, memory constraints, and performance goals. Profiling and benchmarking can further guide decisions by identifying bottlenecks and validating the performance impact of chosen structures. Leveraging built-in libraries and well-tested implementations often accelerates development and ensures reliability.

Data structures profoundly influence the performance of programs by dictating how data is stored, accessed, and manipulated. Understanding the strengths and limitations of different data structures empowers developers to make informed choices that optimize execution time, memory usage, and maintainability. Careful evaluation of application requirements, combined with empirical performance measurements, forms the foundation for effective data structure selection and improved software efficiency.

3.2   Arrays, Lists, and Their Trade-Offs

Arrays and linked lists are among the most fundamental linear data structures used in programming. Both organize data sequentially, allowing elements to be traversed in order. Despite this similarity, arrays and linked lists differ significantly in structure, memory layout, and operational performance. Understanding these differences is crucial for selecting the appropriate structure based on speed requirements, memory constraints, and the nature of data manipulation within an application.

An array represents a collection of elements stored contiguously in a block of memory. Each element is of the same data type and occupies a fixed-size slot within the array. This contiguous allocation enables fast indexed access, allowing any element to be retrieved in constant time, $O(1)$, by calculating its memory address based on the base address and element size. However, arrays have a fixed size defined at the time of creation. Resizing an array generally requires allocating a new larger block of memory and copying elements, which can be expensive for large arrays. In addition, arrays may leave unused allocated space or require resizing strategies such as dynamic arrays to accommodate growth.

Linked lists, on the other hand, consist of nodes where each node contains data and a reference (pointer) to the next node in the sequence. This pointer-based structure does not require contiguous memory, allowing nodes to be scattered throughout the heap. Linked lists support dynamic resizing naturally; inserting or deleting nodes can be done by updating pointers without moving existing data. However, accessing an element by index requires sequential traversal from the head node, resulting in linear time, $O(n)$, for access operations. The additional storage for pointers increases the memory overhead of linked lists compared to arrays.

The table below summarizes the asymptotic time complexity for key operations on arrays and linked lists:

Operation	Array	Linked List
Access by Index	$O(1)$	$O(n)$
Search (unsorted)	$O(n)$	$O(n)$
Insertion (end, if space)	$O(1)$	$O(1)^*$
Insertion (arbitrary position)	$O(n)$	$O(1)$
Deletion (arbitrary position)	$O(n)$	$O(1)$

Table 3.2: *Time complexity comparison of arrays and linked lists*

*Insertion at end for linked list assumes maintaining a tail pointer.

Memory usage differences arise primarily from the storage requirements for pointers in linked lists. Each node in a linked list contains at least one pointer to the next node, increasing the memory consumed compared to arrays, which store only the data elements contiguously without extra metadata per element. This overhead can be significant when the elements themselves are small, such as integers or characters. Arrays also generally exhibit better spatial locality due to contiguous storage, improving cache utilization, while the scattered memory layout of linked lists can result in frequent cache misses, degrading performance on modern processors.

The following table summarizes the key trade-offs between arrays and linked lists:

Arrays	Linked Lists
Fixed size (or costly resize)	Dynamic size, easy resizing
Fast indexed access	Slow, sequential access
Lower memory overhead per element	Higher memory overhead per element (due to pointers)
Better cache locality and performance	Poor cache locality
Insertion and deletion expensive (except at end)	Efficient insertion and deletion when node is known
Suitable for random access scenarios	Suitable for frequent insertions/deletions

Table 3.3: *Comparison of arrays and linked lists*

To illustrate usage differences in practice, consider the following code snippet comparing array and linked list implementations for basic insert and access operations:

```cpp
#include <iostream>
#include <vector> // dynamic array
#include <list>   // linked list

int main() {
    // Dynamic array using vector
    std::vector<int> arr = {1, 2, 3};
```

```
arr.push_back(4); // insert at end
std::cout << "Array element at index 2: " << arr[2] << "\n";

// Linked list
std::list<int> linked_list = {1, 2, 3};
linked_list.push_back(4); // insert at end
auto it = linked_list.begin();
std::advance(it, 2); // move iterator to index 2
std::cout << "List element at position 2: " << *it << "\n";

return 0;
}
```

Basic array and linked list operations

While this example uses standard library implementations for simplicity, it highlights the distinction in accessing elements: arrays provide direct indexing, whereas linked lists require iterator traversal.

The choice between arrays and linked lists has direct implications for algorithm design. Algorithms requiring rapid random access or frequent element retrievals should use arrays to leverage constant-time indexing, improving overall complexity. Conversely, algorithms that must frequently insert or delete elements at arbitrary positions can benefit from linked lists by avoiding costly shifting operations. However, linked lists generally result in higher overhead when frequent searches or indexed access are needed due to traversal requirements, which can degrade performance in large datasets.

To illustrate memory trade-offs concretely, consider measuring memory consumption for a large dataset stored as both an array and a linked list. The following output demonstrates that linked lists consume more memory despite storing the same number of elements, primarily due to pointer overhead:

```
Dataset size: 1,000,000 elements
```

```
Array memory usage: 4,000,000 bytes (4 bytes per int)
Linked list memory usage: 16,000,000 bytes (4 bytes for int + 12 bytes pointe
r overhead per node)
```

This example assumes 4 bytes per integer and approximately 12 additional bytes for pointer(s) per linked list node, depending on platform and implementation. The heightened memory consumption affects cache performance and may increase pressure on system memory.

Selecting the appropriate data structure depends heavily on the intended use case. Arrays excel where fast random access is essential and the size is known or changes infrequently. They are preferable for applications such as image processing, matrix operations, or lookup tables. Linked lists suit environments demanding frequent insertions and deletions where the total size is highly dynamic, such as implementing queues, stacks, or adjacency lists for graphs.

In practice, hybrid structures and abstractions such as dynamic arrays (e.g., vectors) or doubly linked lists combine advantages to meet specific requirements, offering dynamic resizing with efficient insertions and reasonable access performance.

Choosing between arrays and linked lists involves careful consideration of their respective strengths and weaknesses in speed and memory. Understanding these trade-offs helps ensure that software achieves required performance while maintaining manageable resource consumption, ultimately resulting in more reliable and efficient programs.

3.3   Hash Tables, Maps, and Fast Lookup

Hash tables and maps are fundamental data structures widely used to provide efficient data lookup, insertion, and deletion operations. A hash table associates keys with values, enabling rapid retrieval through a process known as hashing. This structure forms the basis of many applications requiring quick data access, such as database indexing, caching, and symbol tables in compilers. Understanding the design, performance characteristics, and trade-offs of hash tables is crucial for implementing performant software.

At the core of a hash table is the hash function, a deterministic algorithm that maps keys of arbitrary type and size to integer indices within a fixed range, typically the size of an underlying array. The hash function calculates an index for each key, enabling direct access to the corresponding value. A simple example of a hash function for string keys might sum the ASCII values of characters modulo the table size.

The following code snippet demonstrates a basic hash function mapping string keys to integer indices:

```
size_t basicHash(const std::string& key, size_t tableSize) {
    size_t hashValue = 0;
    for (char ch : key) {
        hashValue += static_cast<size_t>(ch);
    }
    return hashValue % tableSize;
}
```

This simple function sums the character codes in the key and computes the remainder when divided by the table size, yielding an index in the range $[0, \text{tableSize} - 1]$.

Hash tables aim to offer average-case constant time complexity, $O(1)$, for lookup, insertion, and deletion operations. However, these guarantees depend on minimizing collisions—situations where different keys hash to the same index. The table below summarizes typical time complexities for hash table operations:

Operation	Average Case	Worst Case
Lookup	$O(1)$	$O(n)$
Insertion	$O(1)$	$O(n)$
Deletion	$O(1)$	$O(n)$

Table 3.4: *Time complexity of hash table operations*

Although the worst-case complexity is linear, $O(n)$, due to collisions degrading performance, well-designed hash functions and table management maintain average $O(1)$ complexity.

Collisions occur when distinct keys produce the same hash index. Resolving collisions is critical to preserving hash table performance and correctness. Two common methods are chaining and open addressing.

- **Chaining** involves storing collided elements in a linked list or other container at the indexed slot.

- **Open addressing** resolves collisions by probing alternate slots, using linear probing, quadratic probing, or double hashing to find an empty position.

Chaining simplifies collision management by allowing multiple entries per slot but may incur additional memory overhead due to pointers and fragmentation. Open addressing uses a single array without auxiliary linked structures, often offering better cache performance but requiring careful probing strategies to avoid clustering and maintain efficiency.

As the number of elements in a hash table grows, increased collisions deteriorate performance. To mitigate this, hash tables dynamically resize by allocating a larger array and rehashing existing entries according to the new table size. This process, known as rehashing, involves recomputing the hash indices for all stored keys and redistributing them in the expanded structure.

Rehashing tends to be expensive, running in linear time $O(n)$, but occurs infrequently. Proper load factor thresholds—the ratio of elements to table size—guide when to trigger resizing to balance memory usage and performance. Typically, resizing occurs when the load factor exceeds 0.7 to 0.8, ensuring low collision probability.

Hash tables excel in scenarios requiring fast associative access. Common applications include caches where frequently accessed data is stored for quick retrieval, database indexing to speed up queries, and language runtimes storing variable bindings or symbol tables. Their $O(1)$ average access time makes them preferable over alternatives like trees or lists when order is unimportant and key-based access prevails.

Despite their advantages, hash tables have limitations. They require additional memory over simple arrays or trees due to storage of auxiliary elements such as pointers or empty slots. The choice and quality of the hash function significantly impact collision rates and thus performance. Worst-case access times can degrade to $O(n)$ with poor hash functions or adversarial input, making hash table behavior less predictable. Furthermore, hash tables do not maintain element order, which can be significant for some use cases.

Below is a simple example demonstrating fundamental hash table operations: insertion, lookup, and deletion using a standard associative container in C++.

```cpp
#include <iostream>
#include <unordered_map>
#include <string>

int main() {
    std::unordered_map<std::string, int> hashTable;

    // Insert key-value pairs
    hashTable["apple"] = 3;
    hashTable["banana"] = 5;

    // Lookup
    std::string key = "apple";
    if (hashTable.find(key) != hashTable.end()) {
        std::cout << key << " count: " << hashTable[key] << std::endl;
    } else {
        std::cout << key << " not found.\n";
    }

    // Deletion
    hashTable.erase("banana");

    return 0;
}
```

This code inserts two key-value pairs, retrieves the value for a given key, and removes an entry. The underlying unordered map implements a hash table with effective collision resolution and resizing.

Measuring the performance of hash tables in real applications involves profiling tools and benchmarking approaches. Profilers can reveal hotspots such as excessive hash collisions or long chains that degrade performance. Benchmarks measuring lookup, insertion, and deletion times under varying loads and input distributions inform tuning decisions, including choosing hash functions and load factor thresholds. Instrumenting code to track collision counts and probe lengths further aids optimization.

Optimizing hash functions is pivotal for maximizing hash table efficiency. Effective hash functions produce uniformly distributed output values for a given input domain, reducing collisions. For string keys, algorithms such as MurmurHash, Jenkins hash, or FNV (Fowler–Noll–Vo) are popular due to their speed and distribution quality. Minimizing computational overhead of the hash function is equally important to maintain $O(1)$ operation times.

Good hash function design also considers key domain properties and exploits available randomness. For numerical keys, simple modulo or multiplicative hashing can suffice, while composite keys may require combining hash codes of components carefully.

Hash tables and maps provide powerful data structures for fast key-based data storage and retrieval. Their average-case constant time operations make them indispensable in performance-critical applications. Understanding hashing mechanics, collision resolution, resizing strategies, and hash function optimization is vital for effective use of hash tables. By carefully selecting and tuning these components, developers can build systems that respond efficiently under diverse workloads and scale gracefully.

3.4 Trees and Hierarchical Data

Trees are fundamental data structures in computer science used to represent hierarchical relationships between elements. Unlike linear data structures such as arrays or lists, trees organize data in a branching fashion, where each element, called a node, can have zero or more child nodes. This structure naturally models many real-world systems where entities are arranged in levels or nested relationships, such as file directories, organizational charts, or XML documents. Trees enable efficient organization, search, and manipulation of hierarchical data.

A particularly important variant is the binary search tree (BST), which allows efficient search, insertion, and deletion operations while maintaining sorted order of elements. In a BST, each node contains a key and references to two child nodes—commonly referred to as the left and right subtrees. The BST property requires that all keys in the left subtree are less than the node's key, and all keys in the right subtree are greater. This invariant enables operations like search to traverse the tree by comparing the target key at each node and choosing the appropriate subtree, reducing the search space at every step.

Traversal methods provide systematic ways to visit all nodes in a tree. The three classical traversal orders are in-order, pre-order, and post-order. In in-order traversal, the left subtree is visited first, then the node itself, followed by the right subtree. This order visits nodes in ascending key order for BSTs. Pre-order traversal visits the node before its subtrees, useful for copying or serializing trees. Post-order traversal visits subtrees before the node, appropriate for deleting trees or evaluating expressions. Each traversal has typical use cases depending on the application needs.

The table below summarizes time complexities for search, insertion, and deletion operations in various tree types:

Tree Type	Search	Insertion	Deletion
Binary Search Tree (Average)	$O(\log n)$	$O(\log n)$	$O(\log n)$
Binary Search Tree (Worst)	$O(n)$	$O(n)$	$O(n)$
AVL Tree	$O(\log n)$	$O(\log n)$	$O(\log n)$
Red-Black Tree	$O(\log n)$	$O(\log n)$	$O(\log n)$
B-Tree	$O(\log n)$	$O(\log n)$	$O(\log n)$

Table 3.5: *Time complexity comparison for tree operations*

Plain binary search trees can degenerate into linked lists if insertions are performed in sorted order, leading to worst-case linear-time operations. Balanced trees, such as AVL and Red-Black trees, maintain structural properties to ensure the tree remains approximately balanced after insertions and deletions. Balancing techniques enforce height constraints or coloring rules that restrict the shape of the tree, guaranteeing logarithmic height and thus efficient operations regardless of input order.

The following code snippet illustrates how to implement insertion and search in a binary search tree:

```
struct Node {
    int key;
    Node* left;
    Node* right;
    Node(int k) : key(k), left(nullptr), right(nullptr) {}
};

Node* insert(Node* root, int key) {
    if (!root) return new Node(key);
    if (key < root->key)
        root->left = insert(root->left, key);
    else if (key > root->key)
        root->right = insert(root->right, key);
    return root;
}
```

```
bool search(Node* root, int key) {
    if (!root) return false;
    if (key == root->key) return true;
    if (key < root->key)
        return search(root->left, key);
    else
        return search(root->right, key);
}
```

Trees find widespread use in representing hierarchical data in diverse domains. File systems organize directories and files in tree structures, reflecting nested folders. Database indexes utilize trees such as B-trees to rapidly locate records without scanning entire datasets. Organizational charts present employee hierarchies. Abstract syntax trees model program source code structure in compilers, enabling efficient parsing and analysis.

Despite their advantages, trees introduce trade-offs and limitations. Simple BSTs risk imbalance, degrading operation efficiency. Maintaining balanced trees incurs computational overhead in insertion and deletion to perform rotations or restructuring, increasing implementation complexity. Additionally, pointer-based tree nodes consume extra memory compared to flat arrays. In certain cases, the complexity of balancing algorithms may outweigh benefits for small or static datasets.

Visualizing tree structures aids comprehension of their behavior. Consider a sample BST consisting of the keys 8, 3, 10, 1, 6, 14, 4, 7, and 13:

```
    8
   / \
  3   10
 / \    \
1   6    14
   / \   /
  4   7 13
```

Traversal orders visit nodes in different sequences. The in-order traversal visits: 1, 3, 4, 6, 7, 8, 10, 13, 14. This produces the sorted order of keys inherent to BSTs.

Optimizing tree performance involves selecting appropriate tree types and balancing strategies tailored to application requirements. AVL trees guarantee more rigid balance, resulting in faster lookups at the cost of more rotations during updates. Red-Black trees provide a more relaxed balancing scheme with fewer rotations, often balancing performance and complexity. B-trees extend balancing to multi-way nodes, optimizing disk-based storage by minimizing input/output operations.

When implementing trees, careful consideration of traversal methods, balancing algorithms, and node structures enhances speed and memory usage. Employing iterative implementations, tail recursion, or augmented data can further optimize operations. In read-heavy applications, self-adjusting trees like splay trees adapt to access patterns for improved amortized performance.

Tree data structures are indispensable tools for representing and managing hierarchical data efficiently. Binary search trees and their balanced variants offer logarithmic time operation guarantees, enabling scalable search, insertion, and deletion. Understanding traversal methods, applications, and trade-offs assists developers in effectively leveraging trees to solve complex problems demanding ordered or hierarchical data representation.

3.5   Best Practices and Common Pitfalls

Selecting the appropriate data structure is a foundational step that significantly influences the performance, maintainability, and scalability of software systems. Effective data structure selection requires a thorough assessment of the problem domain, anticipated operations, and usage patterns. Before settling on a specific structure, it is critical to understand the requirements, including the frequency of different operations such as searching, insertion, deletion, and traversal. Moreover, the scale of data and available memory constraints must be considered. This analytical approach guides developers towards choosing data structures that maximize efficiency while meeting functional needs.

One important principle is to avoid premature optimization. Early attempts to optimize data structures based on assumptions rather than empirical evidence can lead to overly complex implementations that may not address actual bottlenecks. Developers should first implement clear, maintainable designs and rely on profiling tools to identify true performance hotspots. Profiling provides objective data about where the application spends time or consumes resources, enabling focused optimizations. This evidence-driven approach ensures effort targets real problems, prevents wasted development time, and maintains code clarity.

Balancing complexity and performance is an essential consideration. While advanced data structures and algorithms might offer impressive theoretical gains, they often increase code complexity, which can introduce bugs, hamper maintainability, and elevate development time. Sometimes a simpler structure with slightly lower performance is preferable to maintain code readability and ease of modification. Moreover, increased complexity may result in greater memory consumption or runtime overhead, negating performance benefits. Striking the right trade-off entails evaluating whether added intricacy justifies expected gains in real-world use.

The following table compares typical memory consumption and access speeds across common data structures, illustrating trade-offs developers must weigh:

Data Structure	Memory Usage	Access Speed
Array	Low	Very Fast (Random Access)
Linked List	Moderate (due to pointers)	Slow (Sequential Access)
Hash Table	High (Metadata and load factor)	Fast (Average $O(1)$)
Binary Search Tree	Moderate	Moderate (Logarithmic)
Balanced Trees (AVL, RB)	Moderate-High	Consistent Logarithmic

Table 3.6: *Memory and speed trade-offs of common data structures*

Testing and profiling data structures is an indispensable practice for making informed choices. Benchmarking code sections with realistic data sets under expected operation distributions offers quantitative insights into performance behavior. The example below demonstrates a simple benchmarking framework in C++ to measure insertion and lookup latency across different data structures:

```cpp
#include <iostream>
#include <chrono>
#include <unordered_map>
#include <map>
#include <vector>

void benchmarkInsertionAndLookup() {
    const int n = 1000000;
    std::vector<int> data(n);
    for (int i = 0; i < n; ++i) data[i] = i;
```

```cpp
std::unordered_map<int, int> umap;
auto start = std::chrono::high_resolution_clock::now();
for (int i : data) umap[i] = i;
auto end = std::chrono::high_resolution_clock::now();
std::cout << "Unordered_map insertion: "
          << std::chrono::duration<double>(end - start).count() << "s
\n";

start = std::chrono::high_resolution_clock::now();
for (int i : data) {
    volatile auto found = umap.find(i);
}
end = std::chrono::high_resolution_clock::now();
std::cout << "Unordered_map lookup: "
          << std::chrono::duration<double>(end - start).count() << "s
\n";

std::map<int, int> omap;
start = std::chrono::high_resolution_clock::now();
for (int i : data) omap[i] = i;
end = std::chrono::high_resolution_clock::now();
std::cout << "Map insertion: "
          << std::chrono::duration<double>(end - start).count() << "s
\n";

start = std::chrono::high_resolution_clock::now();
for (int i : data) {
    volatile auto found = omap.find(i);
}
end = std::chrono::high_resolution_clock::now();
std::cout << "Map lookup: "
          << std::chrono::duration<double>(end - start).count() << "s
\n";
}

int main() {
    benchmarkInsertionAndLookup();
    return 0;
}
```

Benchmarking insertion and search times

Frequent mistakes in data structure selection and implementation can undermine performance significantly. Common errors include neglecting collision resolution in hash tables, which leads to degraded lookup efficiency; failing to balance trees, causing search times to degrade from logarithmic to linear; and choosing linked lists for applications requiring frequent random access. Another pitfall is ignoring memory consumption implications, especially in embedded or memory-constrained environments, which may lead to unexpectedly high resource usage. Awareness and avoidance of these mistakes are crucial for stable, high-performance software.

Improvement in data structure usage often requires iterative refinement, whereby developers repeatedly test, analyze, and modify implementations. The following pseudocode outlines this cyclic process:

```
while (performance not optimal) {
    profile current implementation
    identify bottlenecks related to data structures
    select alternative or optimized data structure
    implement and integrate changes
    validate correctness and performance gains
}
```

Iterative refinement process for data structure optimization

This approach encourages incremental enhancements guided by quantitative feedback rather than guesswork.

Clear documentation and readable code are integral to long-term maintainability of data structure implementations. Thorough comments explaining design decisions, operation complexities, and assumptions help future maintainers and collaborators. Using descriptive naming conventions and modular functions also facilitate understanding, support debugging, and ease integration with other components. Neglecting documentation often results in fragile code that is difficult to optimize or extend.

Real-world case studies illustrate the costly consequences of poor data structure choices. The table below presents examples of software projects where suboptimal data structures led to performance issues, alongside corrective actions taken:

Case	Issue	Resolution
Web Server Cache	Used linked list for cache entries	Replaced with hash table for $O(1)$ lookups, improving response time
Database Indexing	Unbalanced BST causing slow queries	Switched to balanced B-tree, reducing search time from linear to logarithmic
Real-time System	Excessive pointer-heavy structures	Adopted flat arrays to improve cache locality and reduce latency

Table 3.7: *Case studies of data structure-related performance problems*

Adopting best practices in data structure selection and maintenance promotes efficient software capable of meeting evolving performance demands. The checklist below summarizes essential principles:

- Analyze problem requirements thoroughly

- Choose data structures matching operation patterns

- Prioritize maintainability and simplicity

- Use profiling to guide optimizations

- Avoid premature optimizations

- Benchmark with realistic workloads

- Document assumptions and decisions clearly

- Iterate and refine based on data

- Anticipate trade-offs between memory and speed

- Be vigilant about common pitfalls and errors

Incorporating these guidelines within development workflows culti-
vates robust, performant software that leverages data structures effectively while minimizing costly errors and technical debt.

4

Algorithmic Thinking and Complexity

This chapter introduces the fundamental concepts of algorithms and their importance in efficient problem-solving. It covers the significance of analyzing time and space complexity using Big O notation to evaluate algorithm performance. The chapter discusses practical methods for comparing algorithms and making informed choices based on their efficiency. It explores common strategies for algorithm design, such as divide-and-conquer, greedy, and dynamic programming, with illustrative examples. Finally, it provides guidance on identifying and optimizing inefficient patterns to enhance overall program performance.

4.1 What Is an Algorithm?

An *algorithm* is a precise and well-defined set of instructions or rules that describe a step-by-step procedure to solve a specific problem or accomplish a particular task. In computer science and programming, algorithms provide the fundamental framework for writing programs that transform input data into the desired output through a finite sequence of operations. Considered the core of computation, algorithms dictate how a problem is approached, providing a logical sequence that leads from an initial state to a solution.

Effective algorithms do not depend on the programming language or the implementation details but rather on the conceptual steps taken to solve the problem. For example, an algorithm could describe how to sort a list of numbers, search for a particular value within a dataset, or compute mathematical functions such as factorials or Fibonacci numbers. These procedures emphasize clarity, precision, and repeatability, ensuring that for every valid input, the algorithm yields the correct result within a bounded number of steps.

A well-designed algorithm exhibits several key characteristics that distinguish it as a proper computational procedure. First, *correctness* ensures that the algorithm produces the intended output for all valid inputs. Second, *efficiency* relates to the resources the algorithm requires, primarily regarding execution time and memory consumption—both of which should be minimized when possible. Third, *clarity* pertains to the logical simplicity and understandability of the steps, aiding in maintenance and verification. Fourth, *finiteness* guarantees that the algorithm will terminate after a finite number of steps, preventing infinite loops or non-terminating computations. Finally, *determinism* means that the algorithm's behavior is entirely predictable, producing the same output for the same input without randomness or ambiguity.

To illustrate the concept and nature of algorithms, consider the following examples implemented in a commonly used programming language.

```
def linear_search(arr, target):
    for index, value in enumerate(arr):
        if value == target:
            return index
    return -1  # Not found
```

This function implements a basic *linear search* algorithm that sequentially checks each element in an array to find a target value. It exemplifies a simple problem-solving procedure that is easy to understand and correct but may not be optimal for very large datasets.

Another commonly encountered algorithm is the computation of the factorial of a non-negative integer, which demonstrates the use of recursion.

```
def factorial(n):
    if n == 0 or n == 1:
        return 1
    else:
        return n * factorial(n - 1)
```

This recursive algorithm defines factorial in terms of smaller subproblems, highlighting how algorithms can employ self-reference to elegantly reduce complexity.

Sometimes it is beneficial to represent algorithms in a language-agnostic format called *pseudocode*. This form abstracts away syntax details and focuses on the logical flow of the procedure, improving accessibility and aiding reasoning.

```
Algorithm LinearSearch(array A, target T)
    for i = 0 to length(A)-1 do
        if A[i] == T then
            return i
    return -1
```

This pseudocode succinctly captures the critical elements of the linear search algorithm, emphasizing control flow and decision-making.

The role of algorithms in programming tasks extends far beyond mere problem solving. The choice and design of algorithms directly influence software performance, scalability, and complexity. A poorly designed algorithm can lead to excessive execution times, high memory consumption, and maintenance challenges. In contrast, thoughtful algorithm design enhances the user experience by enabling faster responsiveness and effective handling of larger datasets. Moreover, algorithms can embody abstract problem-solving paradigms that facilitate modular design, reusability, and easier debugging.

Ensuring *algorithm correctness* is paramount before optimizing for performance. Correctness means the algorithm must function accurately across all valid inputs, producing reliable and predictable outputs. This requirement often necessitates rigorously verifying boundary cases, input variations, and potential error conditions. Thorough testing, formal proofs, and code reviews are standard practices to achieve correctness, as errors in an algorithm can cascade into significant software faults.

Algorithm design inherently involves trade-offs, principally balancing speed, memory usage, and implementation complexity. For instance, an algorithm that operates rapidly might consume substantial memory, while a memory-efficient solution could run slower. Similarly, the simplest algorithm to implement may not scale efficiently for large

80

data. Understanding these trade-offs enables developers and engineers to make informed decisions aligned with the specific constraints and goals of a project.

Analysis techniques help evaluate the performance and suitability of algorithms before and after implementation. Theoretical analysis provides an abstract view of resource consumption by expressing how the running time or memory demand grows relative to the input size, often using mathematical notation such as Big O. This approach facilitates comparing algorithms on a formal basis, independent of momentary hardware or software conditions. Complementing theoretical insights, empirical analysis involves benchmarking algorithms by measuring their actual execution time and resource use during practical runs. Combining both approaches offers a comprehensive understanding of algorithm behavior and guides optimization efforts.

The impact of algorithm choice becomes evident when comparing several well-known algorithms for a common task such as sorting. The following table summarizes their typical time complexities in average cases and typical space requirements:

Algorithm	Time Complexity (Average Case)	Space Complexity	Comments
Bubble Sort	$O(n^2)$	$O(1)$	Simple but slow for large data
Merge Sort	$O(n \log n)$	$O(n)$	Efficient, stable, uses extra space
Quick Sort	$O(n \log n)$	$O(\log n)$	Very efficient in practice, unstable
Insertion Sort	$O(n^2)$	$O(1)$	Efficient on small or nearly sorted data
Heap Sort	$O(n \log n)$	$O(1)$	Efficient and in-place, unstable

This comparison highlights that while some algorithms like Merge Sort and Quick Sort provide better scalability with larger inputs, they may require additional memory or have other practical considerations. Conversely, simpler algorithms such as Bubble Sort or Insertion Sort, though easier to understand and implement, become inefficient as input size increases.

Overall, understanding what defines an algorithm and its core properties lays the foundation for effective programming. Mastery of algorithmic principles facilitates writing programs that are not only correct but optimized for speed, memory, and maintainability. As software complexity grows, the ability to select and design appropriate algorithms remains crucial for building reliable, scalable, and performant applications that meet user and system requirements.

4.2   Time and Space Complexity Explained

Analyzing the efficiency of algorithms is crucial to understanding their behavior and suitability for specific tasks. Two primary resources consumed by algorithms are time (how long they take to execute) and space (the memory they require during execution). *Time complexity* and *space complexity* formalize these concepts by providing a framework to measure and compare algorithm performance independently of hardware, programming languages, or implementation details.

The most widely used tool for expressing algorithm resource growth is *Big O notation*. Big O conveys how the resource consumption of an algorithm scales as the size of the input increases. Rather than focusing on exact counts of operations or memory units, Big O abstracts growth behavior into categories describing upper bounds on complexity. This abstraction allows programmers and analysts to describe algorithms succinctly and predict their performance on larger inputs.

Formally, Big O notation provides an upper bound on a function's growth rate by ignoring constant factors and lower-order terms. For instance, if an algorithm's running time grows approximately proportional to the square of the input size, it is said to have *quadratic time complexity*, represented as $O(n^2)$. Here, the variable n typically denotes the input size, such as the number of elements in a list or array.

Time complexity measures the number of elementary operations an algorithm performs relative to input size. These operations often include comparisons, assignments, or arithmetic calculations. As input size grows, algorithms vary widely in how quickly their execution time increases. Efficient algorithms exhibit slower growth, enabling them to handle large inputs effectively, whereas inefficient algorithms with rapid growth may become unusable as input size grows.

Similarly, space complexity quantifies the amount of memory an algorithm needs during execution as a function of input size. Some algorithms require only a fixed amount of additional memory regardless of input, classified as $O(1)$ space. Others demand memory proportional to the input, such as $O(n)$, or may even require more complex dependencies. Understanding space complexity helps developers manage resource constraints and optimize programs for environments with limited memory.

Common classifications of Big O notation include the following, with examples for each category:

Complexity	Growth Description	Example Algorithm
$O(1)$	Constant time/space, independent of n	Accessing array element by index
$O(\log n)$	Logarithmic growth	Binary search in a sorted array
$O(n)$	Linear growth	Simple loop over array elements
$O(n \log n)$	Linearithmic growth	Efficient sorting algorithms like Merge Sort
$O(n^2)$	Quadratic growth	Simple sorting algorithms like Bubble Sort

This table summarizes how complexity classes capture increasing rates of growth. Importantly, logarithmic and linearithmic complexities are often acceptable for large inputs, while quadratic or higher orders may become prohibitive as input size grows.

The formal mathematical definition of Big O provides the foundation for these classifications. Given two functions $f(n)$ and $g(n)$ defined on the positive integers, we say that $f(n)$ is $O(g(n))$ if there exist positive constants c and n_0 such that

$$0 \leq f(n) \leq c \cdot g(n), \quad \text{for all} \quad n \geq n_0.$$

This means that beyond some threshold n_0, $f(n)$ does not grow faster than a constant multiple of $g(n)$. This inequality captures the idea of an upper bound on asymptotic growth.

To understand how to derive time complexity, consider the following example of a simple algorithm that computes the sum of all elements in a list:

```
def sum_elements(arr):
    total = 0
    for element in arr:
        total += element
    return total
```

In this algorithm, the loop iterates over each element once, performing a constant-time addition for each. If the input list contains n elements, the number of operations grows linearly with n. Therefore, the time complexity is $O(n)$. The memory usage is $O(1)$ since only a fixed number of variables are used regardless of input size.

Visualizing growth rates helps to grasp the practical impact of complexity differences. Below is a conceptual representation of time complexity functions plotted for increasing input sizes. Note how algorithms with lower order complexity (e.g., $O(\log n)$ or $O(n)$) grow slowly compared to those with higher orders (e.g., $O(n^2)$), which escalate rapidly and become impractical for large n.

Input Size (n)	10	100	1,000	10,000
$O(1)$	1	1	1	1
$O(\log n)$	~3.3	6.6	10	13.3
$O(n)$	10	100	1,000	10,000
$O(n \log n)$	33	660	10,000	133,000
$O(n^2)$	100	10,000	1,000,000	100,000,000

When designing or optimizing algorithms, balancing time and space efficiency is often required. For example, an algorithm that uses additional memory caches intermediate results (space overhead) to reduce repeated computations (time savings). This trade-off between time and space depends on the problem context and resource availability. Prioritizing one resource secondarily to another necessitates careful evaluation of usage patterns and constraints.

Further complexity nuances arise when considering *worst-case, average-case*, and *best-case* scenarios. The worst-case complexity represents the maximum resource consumption over all inputs of size n, offering guarantees about upper bounds. Average-case considers expected performance over a probabilistic distribution of inputs, while best-case reflects minimum effort. The table below exemplifies these cases for common algorithms:

Algorithm	Best Case	Average Case	Worst Case
Linear Search	$O(1)$	$O(n)$	$O(n)$
Binary Search	$O(1)$	$O(\log n)$	$O(\log n)$
Quick Sort	$O(n \log n)$	$O(n \log n)$	$O(n^2)$
Insertion Sort	$O(n)$	$O(n^2)$	$O(n^2)$

Understanding these distinctions assists programmers in anticipating performance variations and preparing for exceptional input cases that might degrade efficiency.

Theoretical analysis through Big O notation must be complemented with *empirical* performance evaluation to gain practical insights. Runtime behavior depends on many factors such as hardware, compiler optimizations, and input data characteristics. Profiling and benchmarking tools help measure actual execution time and memory consumption, enabling validation of theoretical expectations and uncovering real bottlenecks. Both forms of analysis inform informed decisions about algorithm choice, implementation improvements, and resource planning.

Time and space complexity provide formal mechanisms to characterize algorithm performance that remain consistent across environments and inputs. Big O notation simplifies complex behavior into understandable growth classes, while empirical measurements confirm practical applicability. Together, these techniques empower programmers to write efficient, scalable code tailored to problem requirements and system limitations.

4.3 Comparing Algorithms in Practice

While theoretical analysis provides valuable insights into the expected performance of algorithms, practical evaluation through empirical testing and benchmarking is essential for making informed decisions in real-world scenarios. Factors such as hardware architecture, compiler optimizations, input characteristics, and implementation details can significantly influence actual performance and sometimes cause deviations from theoretical predictions. Therefore, assessing algorithms in practice complements theoretical methods by revealing how algorithms behave under specific conditions and workloads.

Benchmarking is a systematic approach to measure the resource usage of different algorithms consistently and fairly. It involves executing each algorithm on a predefined set of test inputs while recording key metrics such as execution time, memory consumption, and scalability. Designing well-structured benchmarks allows developers to identify bottlenecks, quantify improvements, and select the most suitable algorithms for the task at hand.

The following Python example demonstrates a simple benchmarking setup comparing the execution times of two sorting algorithms—built-in sorted() and a naive bubble sort implementation—across identical random inputs.

```
import time
import random

def bubble_sort(arr):
    n = len(arr)
    for i in range(n):
        for j in range(0, n - i - 1):
            if arr[j] > arr[j + 1]:
                arr[j], arr[j + 1] = arr[j + 1], arr[j]
```

```
def benchmark_sorting_algorithms():
    sizes = [100, 500, 1000]
    for size in sizes:
        data = [random.randint(0, 10000) for _ in range(size)]

        # Benchmark built-in sort
        arr_copy = data.copy()
        start = time.perf_counter()
        sorted(arr_copy)
        end = time.perf_counter()
        print(f"Built-in sort for size {size}: {end - start:.6f} seconds
")

        # Benchmark bubble sort
        arr_copy = data.copy()
        start = time.perf_counter()
        bubble_sort(arr_copy)
        end = time.perf_counter()
        print(f"Bubble sort for size {size}: {end - start:.6f} seconds\n
")

if __name__ == "__main__":
    benchmark_sorting_algorithms()
```

This approach uses precise timing functions to capture execution durations and repeats testing for various input sizes to observe performance scaling. Using copies of the same input array ensures consistency across algorithm runs.

Measurement tools extend beyond simple timing calls. Profilers provide detailed information at the function or line level, displaying where the program spends the most time or consumes the most memory. Examples include Python's cProfile for CPU profiling and memory_profiler for monitoring memory usage. Such tools facilitate identifying hotspots in code that could benefit from optimization.

When designing test cases for benchmarking, it is critical to use inputs that are realistic, representative, and diverse. Inputs should reflect the expected workload characteristics, including size ranges, data distributions, and edge cases. For instance, when testing sorting algorithms, inputs can vary from randomly ordered arrays, nearly sorted sequences, reversed lists, or data with many duplicates. This diversity helps evaluate how algorithms perform under different scenarios and how sensitive they are to input characteristics.

Interpreting benchmarking results requires attention to variability and external factors. Multiple runs should be conducted, and average or median values reported to mitigate the effects of transient system loads or background processes. Statistical measures such as standard deviation provide insights into consistency. Additionally, warm-up runs may be necessary to account for just-in-time compilation or caching effects.

Comparative metrics used in algorithm evaluation typically include:

Metric	Measurement	Purpose
Execution Time	Seconds (or milliseconds)	Primary indicator of speed and responsiveness
Memory Usage	Bytes or megabytes	Indicates resource consumption and suitability for limited-memory environments
Scalability	Time/Memory vs. Input Size	Evaluates growth trends and practical limits
Throughput	Operations per unit time	Relevant for streaming or batch processing
Latency	Delay before output	Important in interactive applications

Visualizing results with graphs and charts enhances understanding and communication of comparative performance. Plotting execution time or memory usage against input size reveals differences in growth rates that may be subtle in raw numeric form but critical in practice. The following conceptual output illustrates how a chart might be described in a report:

```
Input Size:      100   500   1000    5000
Built-in Sort:  0.0005 0.0023 0.0050  0.0300
Bubble Sort:    0.0100 0.2500 1.0000  25.0000
```

Such data plotted on a logarithmic scale clearly indicates that built-in sort scales much better than bubble sort as input size increases.

Assessing trade-offs is integral to algorithm selection. While speed is often paramount, other factors such as memory usage, implementation complexity, maintainability, and worst-case performance may influence choices. For example, an algorithm with superior average-case speed but poor worst-case behavior may not be acceptable in safety-critical systems. Similarly, high memory consumption might hinder deployment in constrained environments. Therefore, balancing these aspects according to project requirements ensures an optimal solution.

Real-world case studies exemplify practical algorithm comparison and decision-making. Consider the following instances:

Use Case	Algorithms Compared	Criteria	Outcome
Web Search	Hash Table vs. Balanced Tree	Lookup speed, memory	Hash table chosen for O(1) average lookup
Image Processing	FFT vs. DFT	Execution time, accuracy	FFT selected for efficiency on large inputs
Routing	Dijkstra vs. A*	Pathfinding speed, heuristics	A* preferred with heuristic guidance
Compression	LZW vs. Huffman Coding	Compression ratio, speed	Huffman for simplicity, LZW for better ratio

These case studies demonstrate how context-driven evaluation combining multiple metrics leads to practical algorithm choices.

To conduct reliable, reproducible performance evaluations, adhere to best practices including: isolating testing environments to minimize

90

interference; using fixed random seeds for input generation; running multiple iterations and reporting statistical summaries; documenting benchmarking methodology clearly; and incorporating profiling to complement timing measurements. Automated testing pipelines can further ensure continuous monitoring of algorithm performance during development.

Through the integration of theoretical understanding, empirical benchmarking, and thoughtful analysis, programmers can confidently compare algorithms and select solutions that best fit their application needs, delivering software that performs reliably and efficiently in real deployments.

4.4   Algorithm Design: Strategies and Examples

Designing efficient algorithms is a fundamental skill in programming that enables solving complex problems effectively. Among various approaches to algorithm design, three classical strategies stand out for their wide applicability and proven success: *divide-and-conquer, greedy algorithms,* and *dynamic programming.* Understanding these strategies provides a solid foundation for tackling diverse computational tasks by structuring problem-solving methods based on the problem's nature and constraints.

The *divide-and-conquer* strategy involves decomposing a problem into smaller subproblems of the same type, solving these subproblems independently, and then combining their solutions to construct the solution for the original problem. This recursive approach leverages problem symmetry and reduces complexity by breaking down tasks into manageable units. Divide-and-conquer is especially effective for problems with natural hierarchical or recursive structures.

A classic example of divide-and-conquer is the *merge sort* algorithm, which sorts a list by recursively splitting it into halves, sorting each half, and merging the sorted halves back into a single sorted sequence. This algorithm exhibits efficient performance with a time complexity of $O(n \log n)$, outperforming simpler quadratic methods like bubble sort on large inputs.

The following Python implementation demonstrates merge sort's logic:

```python
def merge_sort(arr):
    if len(arr) <= 1:
        return arr

    mid = len(arr) // 2
    left_half = merge_sort(arr[:mid])
    right_half = merge_sort(arr[mid:])

    return merge(left_half, right_half)

def merge(left, right):
    result = []
    i = j = 0

    while i < len(left) and j < len(right):
        if left[i] <= right[j]:
            result.append(left[i])
            i += 1
        else:
            result.append(right[j])
            j += 1

    result.extend(left[i:])
    result.extend(right[j:])
    return result
```

In contrast to divide-and-conquer, *greedy algorithms* build a solution incrementally by making the locally optimal choice at each step with the hope that these choices lead to a globally optimal solution. Greedy approaches are often simpler and faster but do not guarantee optimality for all problems. When a problem exhibits the *greedy-choice property*, meaning that local optimum choices lead to global optimum results, greedy algorithms become highly effective.

One standard example is the *activity selection problem*, which selects the maximum number of non-overlapping activities from a set of activities with start and finish times. The greedy algorithm sorts activities by their finish times and iteratively picks the earliest finishing activity compatible with the previously selected ones.

Below is a Python example illustrating this greedy approach:

```python
def activity_selection(activities):
    # activities is a list of tuples (start, finish)
    activities.sort(key=lambda x: x[1])  # Sort by finish time

    selected = []
    last_finish = 0

    for activity in activities:
        if activity[0] >= last_finish:
            selected.append(activity)
            last_finish = activity[1]

    return selected
```

Unlike greedy algorithms, *dynamic programming* solves problems by breaking them into overlapping subproblems and solving each subproblem once, storing its result for future use. This technique avoids redundant computations and exploits problem structure where subproblems recur multiple times. Dynamic programming typically applies to optimization problems exhibiting *optimal substructure* and *overlapping subproblems*.

An instructive example is the computation of Fibonacci numbers, where a naive recursive implementation recalculates many values multiple times. Using dynamic programming with *memoization* caches computed results, significantly improving efficiency.

The following code demonstrates Fibonacci computation using dynamic programming:

```
def fibonacci(n, memo=None):
    if memo is None:
        memo = {}
    if n <= 1:
        return n
    if n not in memo:
        memo[n] = fibonacci(n-1, memo) + fibonacci(n-2, memo)
    return memo[n]
```

In this approach, previously computed Fibonacci numbers are stored in a dictionary, preventing repeated calculations and reducing exponential time complexity to linear.

Comparing these strategies highlights their distinct characteristics and typical use cases. The table below summarizes key properties of divide-and-conquer, greedy, and dynamic programming approaches:

Strategy	Approach	Use Cases	Key Characteristics
Divide-and-Conquer	Recursive subdivision	Sorting, searching, FFT	Breaks problem into independent subproblems
Greedy	Locally optimal choices	Scheduling, Huffman coding	Fast, simple, may be suboptimal
Dynamic Programming	Reuse overlapping subproblems	Optimization, sequence alignment	Efficient for overlapping subproblems

Choosing the appropriate strategy depends on the problem's nature. To aid this selection, consider the following questions as a checklist:

94

- Can the problem be divided into smaller independent subproblems? (Consider divide-and-conquer)

- Does a sequence of local choices lead to a globally optimal solution? (Consider greedy)

- Are there overlapping subproblems and can storing intermediate results avoid redundant computations? (Consider dynamic programming)

- What are the constraints on time, memory, and implementation complexity?

- Are exact optimal solutions necessary, or are approximations acceptable?

Understanding the performance trade-offs among these strategies is crucial. Divide-and-conquer algorithms often provide optimal asymptotic performance but may require additional memory for recursion and merging. Greedy algorithms tend to be the simplest to implement and fastest in practice but are limited to certain problem classes. Dynamic programming provides efficient solutions to complex problems but can consume significant memory for caching and may have less intuitive implementations.

In practice, a hybrid approach sometimes yields the best results, applying divide-and-conquer for high-level structure and dynamic programming or greedy methods within subproblems. Evaluating these trade-offs with regard to problem size, resource availability, and correctness criteria leads to effective, maintainable algorithm design.

Ultimately, mastering these classical strategies equips programmers with versatile tools to analyze problems critically, devise efficient solutions, and understand the underlying trade-offs that impact program performance and maintainability.

4.5   Spotting and Fixing Inefficient Patterns

Inefficient coding patterns frequently lead to degraded program performance, especially as data sizes grow or as software complexity increases. Common contributors to slow execution include deeply nested loops, redundant calculations performed repeatedly, unnecessary data copying, and misuse of data structures. Recognizing these patterns is a critical step toward writing faster code and optimizing existing implementations.

One prevalent inefficiency arises from nested loops with high iteration counts, often resulting in quadratic or worse time complexity. For example, a double loop iterating over all pairs in a list of size n yields $O(n^2)$ runtime, which can become impractical for large inputs. Similarly, recomputing values inside loops rather than caching results inflates execution time unnecessarily. Copying large datasets or objects inside loops instead of manipulating references also incurs avoidable overhead. Awareness of such structural inefficiencies enables developers to target bottlenecks effectively.

Detecting slow patterns requires systematic examination of code logic and runtime behavior. Static code analysis may reveal explicit nested iterations and repeated expressions, whereas dynamic profiling tools provide empirical evidence by monitoring execution hotspots. Profilers instrument code to measure the time or resources consumed by functions or specific code lines, allowing precise localization of performance concerns.

The following Python snippet uses the built-in `cProfile` module to profile a function suspected of being slow:

```
import cProfile

def example_function():
    total = 0
    for i in range(10000):
        for j in range(10000):
            total += i * j
    return total

if __name__ == "__main__":
    cProfile.run('example_function()')
```

Running this profiler outputs detailed statistics on function call counts and execution times, pinpointing where most runtime is spent. This guided insight directs optimization efforts toward the most impactful code sections.

Refactoring inefficient code involves applying strategies to reduce complexity and resource use. One common technique is replacing nested loops with data structures enabling faster lookup or aggregation. For instance, transforming an $O(n^2)$ pairwise search into a linear-time hash-based membership check can dramatically enhance speed. Removing redundant calculations through memoization or precomputation also improves efficiency. Furthermore, minimizing data copying by using in-place operations or references reduces memory overhead and execution time.

The following pseudocode illustrates replacing a nested loop searching for matching pairs with a more efficient hash-based approach:

```
Original Nested Loop:
for each element A in list1:
    for each element B in list2:
        if A == B:
```

```
            process match

Optimized Hash Lookup:
create a hash set H containing elements of list2
for each element A in list1:
    if A in H:
        process match
```

This substitution reduces time complexity from quadratic to near linear by leveraging hashing.

Practical optimization often leads to substantial performance gains as demonstrated by before-and-after measurements. Consider an initial nested loop implementation versus a refactored version using a hash set. Timing results may look as follows:

```
Before optimization:
Input size: 10,000
Execution time: 60 seconds

After optimization:
Input size: 10,000
Execution time: 0.5 seconds
```

Such dramatic improvements underscore the value of identifying inefficient patterns and applying appropriate refactoring.

Adopting best practices from the start helps avoid common performance pitfalls. Writing clear, modular code facilitates reasoning about efficiency. Choosing appropriate data structures aligned with access patterns prevents unnecessary overhead. Avoiding premature optimization focuses efforts on critical bottlenecks rather than microoptimizations. Regular use of profiling during development guides timely detection of inefficiencies before they escalate.

Inefficient Pattern	Suggested Fix
Deeply nested loops	Use hashing, indexing, or set operations
Redundant calculations inside loops	Cache results, use memoization
Unnecessary data copying	Use references or in-place modification
Unbalanced recursion	Convert to iterative or memoized solutions
Inefficient data structures	Use suitable containers (hash tables, heaps)

A systematic approach to optimization can be modeled as the following sequence of steps, presented here in pseudocode flowchart form:

```
Start
  |
  V
Identify suspicious code (profiling, code review)
  |
  V
Analyze complexity and data flows
  |
  V
Locate bottlenecks and inefficient patterns
  |
  V
Formulate optimization strategy (refactor, restructure)
  |
  V
Implement changes
  |
  V
Test for correctness and performance improvement
  |
  V
Repeat as necessary or conclude
```

Finally, thorough testing and validation are essential to ensure that performance improvements do not compromise correctness or introduce inconsistencies. Unit tests should verify that outputs remain accurate post-refactoring. Benchmark tests comparing before-and-after runtimes confirm performance gains. Regression tests guard against unintended side effects. Continuous integration of these practices fosters stable, efficient software development.

By vigilantly identifying inefficient patterns, leveraging profiling tools, applying targeted refactoring methods, and validating results, programmers can enhance algorithmic efficiency and create faster, more resource-friendly applications.

5

Memory Management and Optimization

This chapter explores how programs utilize memory, including stack, heap, and static storage, and the implications for performance. It discusses different memory management models, such as manual allocation and automatic garbage collection, highlighting their trade-offs. Common memory issues like leaks, fragmentation, and dangling references are examined, along with strategies to mitigate them. Techniques for reducing memory footprint, including data compression and efficient data structures, are covered. The chapter concludes with methods for leveraging caching and buffering to enhance speed and improve locality of reference.

5.1 How Programs Use Memory

Programs rely on different memory regions to store data during their execution, and understanding these memory segments is fundamental to writing efficient and robust software. The primary memory areas used by most programs are the stack, the heap, and static storage. Each serves distinct purposes and operates under different constraints, influencing how data is allocated, accessed, and managed.

The **stack** is a region of memory that supports *last-in, first-out* (LIFO) allocation, primarily used for managing function call frames, local variables, and control flow information such as return addresses. When a function is called, a stack frame is created at the top of the stack containing the function's local data and bookkeeping information. When the function returns, its frame is popped from the stack, and control resumes at the calling location. The size of the stack is typically limited and fixed, which confines the amount of memory available for local variables. Stack allocations are fast due to their simple push/pop behavior.

In contrast, the **heap** is a large, dynamically managed memory area intended for data whose size or lifetime cannot be predetermined at compile time. Objects or data structures with variable size or lifespan that extends beyond a single function call are allocated on the heap. Unlike the stack, memory on the heap is manually or automatically allocated and freed, depending on the programming language and memory management model. Heap allocation involves managing free and used memory blocks, which introduces overhead and potential fragmentation but provides the flexibility necessary for complex data handling.

102

Static storage refers to memory allocated for global variables, static variables within functions, and constants that exist for the entire lifetime of the program. This area is reserved at program startup and remains allocated until the program terminates. Because static data is fixed and persistent, it provides a reliable means to store information accessible throughout the program's execution, such as configuration settings or program-wide counters.

To illustrate the differences, consider a program's memory layout during execution. At the low end of the address space, static storage holds global and static variables. Above this resides the heap, which grows upwards as dynamic memory is allocated. At the high end, the stack grows downwards with each function call. This layout helps prevent overlap, allowing separate and efficient management of different types of data.

Function call frames on the stack contain information such as parameters, local variables, saved registers, and the return address. Because stack allocation is implicit and automatic, programmers need not explicitly allocate or free memory for local variables; the runtime handles this as functions enter and exit. For example, recursive functions rely heavily on stack frames, and excessive recursion depth can exhaust the stack, causing a stack overflow. The constrained size and fast access time of the stack make it ideal for temporary, short-lived data needing rapid access.

Heap memory allocation provides the flexibility to create data structures that persist beyond a single function call or whose size varies at runtime. Languages like C provide functions such as `malloc` and `free` for manual heap management, while higher-level languages may use automatic memory management techniques such as garbage collection. Heap allocation is slower than stack allocation because it involves nav-

103

igation through meta-data to find suitable free memory blocks and updating data structures managing free space. Additionally, heap memory can become fragmented over time, meaning free memory is broken into small pieces that may not be usable for large allocations, potentially degrading performance.

Global and static variables stored in static memory have fixed addresses accessible throughout the program. These variables facilitate communication across different parts of the program and retain their values between function calls. Because of their permanence and global scope, static variables should be used judiciously to avoid unintended side effects and maintain code modularity.

The following example code in C demonstrates allocation in each segment:

```c
#include <stdio.h>
#include <stdlib.h>

// Static storage: global variable
static int static_counter = 0;

void function_example() {
    // Stack allocation: local variables
    int local_var = 10;

    // Heap allocation: dynamic memory
    int* heap_var = (int*) malloc(sizeof(int));
    if (heap_var == NULL) {
        printf("Heap allocation failed\n");
        return;
    }
    *heap_var = 20;

    printf("Static: %d, Local: %d, Heap: %d\n", static_counter, local_var
    , *heap_var);

    // Deallocate heap memory
    free(heap_var);
```

```
}

int main() {
    static_counter = 5;
    function_example();
    return 0;
}
```

During execution, the program's memory layout can be visualized as follows:

Stack (grows →)
Function frames
Local variables
Heap (grows ↑)
Dynamically allocated data and objects
Static Storage (fixed)
Global variables
Static variables
Constants

Understanding how memory is organized aids in grasping the performance implications. Stack allocation benefits from spatial locality and simplified management, resulting in low latency and minimal overhead. However, limited size and automatic lifetime restrict its use. Heap allocation is flexible but can incur latency due to search and bookkeeping operations, and improper management risks fragmentation and memory leaks. Static storage access times are generally stable, but excessive use can increase a program's memory footprint unnecessarily.

Different programming languages approach memory management in diverse ways. The following table summarizes typical behavior regarding stack, heap, and static storage management across several common languages:

Language	Stack Usage	Heap Usage	Static Storage Usage
C/C++	Manual stack for local vars	Manual heap allocation	Global/static variables
Java	Stack for primitives/local refs	Heap for objects	Static class variables
Python	Stack frames for calls	Heap for all objects	Module-level globals/consts
Rust	Stack for locals	Heap via Box and other types	Static/globals
Go	Stack automatically managed	Heap for closures, slices	Package-level vars

Incorrect memory handling can lead to issues such as memory leaks and fragmentation. A *memory leak* occurs when a program allocates memory but fails to release it after use, gradually exhausting available memory and leading to degraded performance or crashes. Fragmentation is the deterioration of contiguous free memory into scattered smaller blocks, complicating allocation of large objects. Both are challenges especially prevalent in manual memory management environments but can also occur with automatic models if references are retained inadvertently.

Effective memory usage involves several best practices:

- Always pair each memory allocation with a corresponding deallocation or rely on automatic management.

- Minimize lifetime and scope of variables.

- Avoid unnecessary duplication of data.

- Use appropriate data structures tailored to the memory requirements of the application.

Tools like memory profilers and sanitizers assist in detecting leaks and improper memory access.

By mastering the distinctions and applications of stack, heap, and static storage, programmers can write software that balances performance, efficiency, and reliability. Recognizing how these memory areas operate under the hood supports improved debugging, optimization, and resource management throughout the development lifecycle.

5.2 Memory Management Models

Memory management is a foundational aspect of programming that determines how a program acquires, uses, and releases memory during its execution. Two predominant models exist for managing memory: manual memory management and automatic garbage collection. These models differ in how memory allocation and deallocation are performed, impacting program safety, complexity, and performance.

Manual memory management requires the programmer to explicitly request memory allocation and handle its release when it is no longer needed. This approach is characteristic of languages such as C and C++. Developers use functions like `malloc` or `new` to allocate memory on the heap and must invoke `free` or `delete` to release that memory. This explicit control allows precise management of resources but demands careful attention to avoid errors such as memory leaks, where allocated memory is never freed, or dangling pointers, where references persist after their target memory has been released.

Consider the following conceptual pseudocode demonstrating manual management:

1: $ptr \leftarrow$ AllocateMemory(size)
2: **if** `ptr` is not `null` **then**
3:     Use memory at `ptr`

4:    FREEMEMORY(`ptr`)

5: **end if**

The programmer is responsible for calling `AllocateMemory` and ensuring that every allocated block is deallocated exactly once to avoid resource leaks or premature deallocation. Because of this, manual memory management allows for fine-grained control over memory usage patterns, potentially leading to optimized performance and minimal overhead. Developers can tailor allocation strategies and reuse memory efficiently, which can be critical in high-performance or resource-constrained systems.

However, manual memory management increases programming complexity and the risk of subtle bugs. Memory leaks reduce available memory over time, leading to degraded application performance or crashes. Dangling pointers create undefined behavior, potentially causing data corruption or security vulnerabilities. The cognitive overhead of tracking every allocation and deallocation can slow development and make maintenance challenging.

Automatic garbage collection is the alternative model used by many modern languages including Java, C#, Python, and JavaScript. In this paradigm, the runtime system automatically detects when memory is no longer in use—that is, when there are no reachable references to objects—and reclaims it without programmer intervention. This is typically achieved through mechanisms such as reference counting, tracing collectors, or generational garbage collection.

A simplified pseudocode to illustrate garbage collection is as follows:

1: **while** true **do**

2:    Detect objects with no reachable references

3:    Deallocate detected objects

4:    Execute program instructions
5: **end while**

The automation provided by garbage collection substantially improves software reliability by eliminating many common errors associated with manual memory management. Programmers need not explicitly free memory, which reduces the risks of leaks and dangling pointers and simplifies code structure. This results in increased safety and developer productivity.

Nevertheless, garbage collection introduces trade-offs. Automatic reclamation requires periodic pauses to identify and free unused memory, which can produce unpredictable latency, or *stop-the-world* pauses, detrimental in real-time or low-latency applications. Additionally, garbage collectors consume processing resources, potentially increasing CPU usage and memory overhead compared to manual management. The nondeterministic timing of deallocation can complicate resource management involving external resources such as file handles or network connections.

The following table compares critical characteristics of manual memory management and automatic garbage collection:

Characteristic	Manual Memory Management	Automatic Garbage Collection
Control	Programmer explicitly allocates and frees memory	Runtime system manages memory lifecycle
Safety	Prone to leaks, dangling pointers, and errors	Reduces memory-related bugs and leaks
Performance	Potentially faster with less overhead	Overhead due to periodic collection cycles
Development Complexity	Higher; requires careful bookkeeping	Lower; simplifies programming model
Latency	Predictable; deallocation occurs immediately	May introduce unpredictable pause times
Debugging	Memory bugs difficult to detect and fix	Easier detection of memory-related issues
Real-time Suitability	Well-suited due to deterministic behavior	Challenging due to GC pauses

Understanding these differences is crucial for selecting the appropriate memory management model according to the project's requirements and constraints.

To demonstrate manual memory management more concretely, consider the following pseudocode that explicitly manages heap memory:

```
1: function ProcessData
2:     data ← AllocateMemory(size)
3:     if data is null then
4:         Handle allocation failure
5:         return
6:     end if
7:     Use data for processing
8:     FreeMemory(data)
9: end function
```

In this workflow, allocation and deallocation are paired explicitly within the same function or call chain. The correctness of this pattern directly affects the program's stability and resource usage.

110

Conversely, the garbage-collected model allows code without explicit deallocation:

```
1: function PROCESSDATA
2:     data ← ALLOCATEMEMORY(size)
3:     if data is null then
4:         Handle allocation failure
5:         return
6:     end if
7:     Use data for processing
8:     // No explicit free needed; GC will reclaim
9: end function
```

Here, the runtime periodically traverses the object graph, identifies that data is no longer reachable after the function ends, and frees the associated memory asynchronously.

Performance considerations are paramount when choosing between these models. Manual memory management can deliver high performance by reducing runtime overhead and allowing developers to optimize allocation patterns. However, the additional risk of memory errors can offset these gains by increasing debugging time and introducing instability. Garbage collection improves code safety and maintainability at the cost of additional CPU usage and unpredictable latency, which may be unacceptable in performance-critical or real-time systems.

Many modern languages and environments attempt to balance these trade-offs using hybrid approaches. For example, Rust employs a compile-time ownership system that enforces memory safety without a runtime garbage collector. Some managed runtimes allow manual memory management within controlled scopes or provide real-time garbage collectors with minimized pause times.

Manual memory management grants developers full control but demands vigilance and expertise to avoid serious errors and inefficiencies, while automatic garbage collection abstracts these responsibilities at the expense of performance overhead and timing unpredictability. Selecting the appropriate model requires evaluating the application's priorities, developer skill set, and runtime environment, forming a fundamental decision in designing efficient and reliable software systems.

5.3   Common Memory Problems

Memory management errors can severely impact the stability, security, and performance of software applications. Despite advances in programming languages and environments, common memory problems such as memory leaks, fragmentation, and dangling references persist and continue to challenge developers. Understanding these issues and applying effective strategies to detect and mitigate them is essential for reliable and efficient programming.

A **memory leak** occurs when a program allocates memory but fails to release it after use. This means that the memory remains reserved by the running process and is no longer accessible or needed. As leaks accumulate over time, the program's available memory decreases, potentially resulting in degraded performance, excessive paging to disk, or even application crashes. Memory leaks are especially problematic in long-running processes such as servers, where unreleased allocations steadily exhaust system resources.

Memory leaks arise most commonly in manual memory management environments such as C and C++, where the programmer is responsible for explicitly freeing allocated memory. However, leaks can also occur in garbage-collected languages when references to unused objects are inadvertently retained, preventing the collector from reclaiming them.

The following example, written in C, illustrates a typical memory leak caused by forgetting to free dynamically allocated memory:

```c
void create_leak() {
    int* numbers = (int*) malloc(100 * sizeof(int));
    if (numbers == NULL) {
        // Allocation failed, handle error
        return;
    }
    // Use numbers for computation

    // Missing free; the allocated memory is never released
}
```

In this code, `malloc` allocates a block of memory, but the function omits the call to `free`. Each time `create_leak` is invoked, additional memory is lost, compounding the problem.

Memory fragmentation describes the condition where free memory is divided into many small, noncontiguous blocks, making it difficult to allocate large contiguous regions despite having enough total free memory. Fragmentation primarily affects the heap, where dynamic allocations and deallocations occur at varying sizes and times. Over prolonged execution, allocations of different sizes scattered across the heap create gaps that cannot be merged efficiently.

Fragmentation reduces memory utilization efficiency and can increase allocation time, as the allocator searches for suitable regions large enough to fulfill requests. Severe fragmentation may cause allocation failures even when sufficient total memory exists. This phenomenon is particularly critical in systems with limited memory resources or real-time constraints.

A simple visualization of fragmentation over time may look as follows:

```
Time 0: |AAAAAAA|BBBBBBB|CCCCCCC| (Contiguous allocations)
Time 1: |AAAA_AA|__BBBB_|CCCC_CC| (Some blocks freed)
Time 2: |AA_A_AA|__B__B_|C___CC_| (Fragmented free spaces, no large block)
```

Here, underscores represent free space; fragmented small gaps hinder allocating larger blocks.

To detect memory leaks, developers commonly use profiling tools and specialized analyzers. Tools such as Valgrind's memcheck on Linux, Visual Studio's memory profiler, or built-in diagnostic utilities in managed runtimes can identify leaks by tracking allocations and verifying that all have matching deallocation. These tools report unreleased memory blocks, often with stack traces where allocations occurred, facilitating precise debugging.

Addressing fragmentation requires strategies geared toward more predictable memory usage. One approach is *memory pooling*, where fixed-size blocks are pre-allocated and reused, reducing fragmentation by limiting dynamic size variations. Another method is *compaction*, performed by some garbage collectors, which moves live objects together to create larger contiguous free regions. While compaction can improve allocation efficiency, it requires updating all references to moved objects, adding runtime overhead.

Dangling references or *dangling pointers* occur when a pointer refers to memory that has already been freed or released. Accessing such pointers results in undefined behavior, including crashes, incorrect data, or

114

security vulnerabilities such as use-after-free attacks. Dangling pointers are a common cause of subtle and hard-to-reproduce bugs.

To safely handle pointers and mitigate dangling references, best practices include nullifying pointers immediately after freeing the associated memory and never using pointers after deallocation. In languages that support it, advanced techniques such as smart pointers (e.g., `std::unique_ptr` and `std::shared_ptr` in C++) automate ownership tracking and deallocation, drastically reducing the risk of dangling pointers.

Ensuring memory safety also benefits from disciplined design patterns like RAII (Resource Acquisition Is Initialization), where resource allocation and deallocation are tied to object lifetime, ensuring deterministic cleanup. Regular memory audits, code reviews, and dynamic analysis tools further reinforce safe practices by identifying questionable memory ownership or usage.

Overall, managing memory effectively involves a multifaceted approach: proactively preventing leaks by releasing memory timely, minimizing fragmentation via suitable allocation strategies, and avoiding dangling references through careful pointer management. Employing modern tools to monitor and verify memory usage facilitates early detection of issues, reducing bugs and improving program robustness.

By recognizing and addressing these common memory problems, developers can build software that maintains stability and performs consistently, even under demanding workloads or extended operation.

5.4   Reducing Memory Footprint

Efficient memory usage is a critical priority in software development, especially in environments with limited resources such as embedded systems, mobile devices, or applications requiring high scalability. Reducing the memory footprint of a program not only conserves resources but can also improve performance by enhancing cache utilization and reducing page faults. Several techniques exist to minimize memory consumption while carefully balancing the impact on speed, accuracy, and code complexity.

One broad category of approaches focuses on *data compression*, which reduces the size of data by encoding it more concisely. Compression methods are generally divided into *lossless* and *lossy* techniques. Lossless compression preserves all original data exactly, enabling perfect reconstruction at decompression. Popular lossless algorithms include Huffman coding, run-length encoding, and Lempel-Ziv variants. These are vital in scenarios where data integrity is essential, such as executable files, textual data, or configuration parameters.

Lossy compression, by contrast, sacrifices some fidelity to achieve higher compression ratios, typically applied in multimedia domains such as images, audio, and video. In these cases, minor inaccuracies are acceptable or even imperceptible to users. Examples include JPEG for images or MP3 for audio. When employing lossy compression, developers must weigh the trade-off between reduced memory usage and acceptable distortion.

Beyond compressing data at rest or during transmission, programs can implement compression on in-memory data structures when feasible. This may involve transforming data into a compact encoded form and

116

decoding on access. Techniques like run-length encoding can be applied to sequences with repeated values, minimizing storage for uniform data.

An illustrative example in C demonstrates a simple run-length encoding (RLE) scheme for compressing a sequence of characters:

```c
void rle_encode(const char* input, char* output) {
    int count = 1;
    while (*input) {
        char current = *input;
        int run_length = 1;
        while (input[run_length] == current && run_length < 255) {
            run_length++;
        }
        *output++ = current;
        *output++ = run_length;  // Store run length as a byte
        input += run_length;
    }
    *output = '\0';
}
```

This function converts sequences like "aaaabbbc" into a compressed format storing the character followed by its repetition count, substantially reducing memory usage for repeated data.

Another technique that directly optimizes memory usage involves *structure packing*. Many programming languages and architectures align data structures in memory according to certain boundaries (e.g., 4-byte or 8-byte boundaries). This alignment facilitates faster access but sometimes leads to padding bytes inserted between fields, inflating the size of the structure unnecessarily.

By packing structures to eliminate or minimize padding, programmers can reduce wasted space. In C and C++, compiler-specific directives or attributes exist to control packing behavior. For example:

```
typedef struct __attribute__((packed)) {
    char flag;          // 1 byte
    int count;          // 4 bytes, no padding applied
    short code;         // 2 bytes
} PackedStruct;
```

When packed, this structure occupies exactly 7 bytes rather than being rounded up to 12 bytes due to alignment padding. While structure packing can reduce memory consumption, it may increase access time on some architectures because of unaligned memory accesses, thus requiring careful evaluation.

In addition to compression and packing, designing *memory-efficient algorithms* is fundamental to minimizing runtime memory usage. Some algorithms are specifically crafted to process data incrementally or stream data without loading the entire dataset into memory. For instance, streaming algorithms calculate aggregates or detect patterns on-the-fly, greatly reducing peak memory requirements.

Dynamic programming algorithms can also be optimized to use less memory by retaining only necessary data rather than storing full tables. Similarly, succinct data structures represent information using near-minimal space while supporting efficient queries—important in applications like search engines or databases.

Consider the following hypothetical performance comparison of a traditional algorithm versus its memory-optimized version:

Algorithm	Peak Memory Usage	Execution Time
Standard	100 MB	5 s
Optimized	25 MB	6.5 s

Here, the optimized algorithm reduces memory usage by 75% at the expense of a moderate execution time increase, acceptable in many real-world scenarios.

When employing memory reduction techniques, it is essential to consider trade-offs. Data compression may introduce decompression overhead, affecting responsiveness. Structure packing can increase CPU cycles due to unaligned access penalties. Memory-efficient algorithms may be more complex to implement and maintain, potentially diminishing developer productivity or introducing bugs. Lossy compression involves an accuracy sacrifice, which may be unacceptable in certain applications.

Best practices to minimize memory footprint include reusing existing data structures and references to avoid data duplication, choosing the smallest appropriate data types (such as `uint8_t` instead of `int` where possible), and selecting data structures that suit operational patterns—e.g., arrays for dense data and linked lists for variable-sized collections when memory is fragmented.

Leveraging high-level language features and libraries optimized for low memory consumption can also aid developers. Profiling memory usage during development identifies hotspots and informs targeted optimization, enabling an iterative approach to refining footprint while preserving performance and maintainability.

Through the thoughtful application of data compression, structure packing, and memory-aware algorithm design, programmers can significantly reduce the memory footprint of their applications, ultimately improving efficiency and scalability in a resource-constrained world.

5.5   Caching and Buffering Techniques

Optimizing program performance often involves managing how data is accessed and transferred within the system. Two fundamental techniques to achieve this are *caching* and *buffering*. Both serve to reduce latency and improve throughput by exploiting different properties of hardware and input/output (I/O) operations.

Caching involves storing copies of frequently accessed data in faster, closer storage to the processor, significantly reducing the time it takes to retrieve that data on subsequent accesses. By keeping recently used or nearby data readily available, caches minimize the need to access slower main memory or storage devices. Buffering, on the other hand, smooths out temporary differences in data production and consumption rates by aggregating data into blocks before processing or transmission. This reduces the overhead of costly I/O operations and enables more efficient use of system resources.

The efficiency of caching relies largely on **locality principles**. *Temporal locality* refers to the likelihood that recently accessed data will be accessed again soon. Programs often repeatedly use the same variables or data structures within a short time frame, making caching of those items beneficial. *Spatial locality* describes the tendency to access data located near previously accessed memory addresses. For example, iterating over an array accesses elements stored contiguously, favoring cache lines that are loaded entirely. Efficient cache utilization depends on leveraging these locality properties to reduce cache misses, where requested data is not found in the cache.

Modern processors implement multiple levels of caches that differ in size, speed, and proximity to the CPU cores. The following table summarizes key characteristics of typical CPU cache levels and other common caches:

Cache Level	Size	Latency	Typical Usage
L1 Cache	~32 KB	1–3 CPU cycles	Closest to core; split into instruction and data caches
L2 Cache	~256 KB to 512 KB	10–20 CPU cycles	Shared per core or per cluster; larger but slower
L3 Cache	Several MBs	30–60 CPU cycles	Shared among cores; larger but slowest on-chip cache
Disk Cache (OS)	Several MBs/GB	Milliseconds	Caches disk blocks in RAM
Web Cache	Varies	Milliseconds to seconds	Stores network content for reuse

Each cache level serves as a buffer to its next outer layer, bridging speed gaps between CPU registers, memory, and storage. The hierarchy enables a balance between fast access and sufficient capacity.

Buffering is commonly used in I/O operations such as file reading/writing and network communication. Instead of processing data byte by byte, programs accumulate data into buffers, which are blocks of memory holding data temporarily before consumption or transfer. Buffering reduces the number of system calls and interactions with slower peripherals, leveraging the bursty nature of I/O to maximize throughput.

For instance, buffered file I/O reads a large chunk of data into memory once and then serves smaller requests from the buffer, reducing the overhead associated with frequent disk reads. Similarly, network buffers aggregate packets before sending or after receiving, smoothing variable transmission rates and avoiding congestion.

Implementing cache-aware algorithms entails carefully structuring

121

data access patterns to prefetch data into caches before it is needed. Consider the following simplified C-style code snippet that preloads data to utilize caching effectively:

```
void process_array(int* array, size_t size) {
    for (size_t i = 0; i < size; i += 16) {
        __builtin_prefetch(&array[i + 16], 0, 3);
        // Process elements in current cache line
        for (size_t j = i; j < i + 16 && j < size; ++j) {
            array[j] = array[j] * 2;
        }
    }
}
```

This code uses a compiler intrinsic to hint the processor to load the next cache line into L1 cache in advance, reducing stalls caused by cache misses as the processing loop advances.

Buffering in I/O can be demonstrated by reading a file in blocks rather than byte-by-byte, as shown:

```
#define BUFFER_SIZE 4096

void read_file(const char* filename) {
    FILE* file = fopen(filename, "rb");
    if (!file) return;

    char buffer[BUFFER_SIZE];
    size_t bytesRead;

    while ((bytesRead = fread(buffer, 1, BUFFER_SIZE, file)) > 0) {
        // Process buffer contents
    }

    fclose(file);
}
```

By reading data in buffers, the program minimizes the number of expensive read operations, resulting in faster overall performance.

The performance improvements from effective caching are quantifiable. Programs that optimize their data structures and access patterns to exploit cache locality often experience reduced latency and increased execution speed. For example, a matrix multiplication optimized for cache usage may execute multiple times faster than a naïve implementation due to fewer cache misses and reduced memory access time.

Despite the substantial benefits, caching and buffering introduce trade-offs and limitations. Cache invalidation occurs when cached data becomes stale due to underlying data changes, necessitating mechanisms to maintain coherence, especially in multicore or distributed systems. Cache coherence protocols add complexity and overhead to preserve consistency across caches.

Buffer overflows—when data exceeds buffer boundaries—are a classic source of program errors and security vulnerabilities. Proper buffer size management and bounds checking are essential to avoid such defects. Additionally, inappropriate buffer sizes can lead to memory waste or degraded performance; buffers too small increase overhead, while excessively large buffers consume unnecessary memory.

Best practices for caching and buffering include designing software with cache-friendly data structures such as arrays over linked lists to maximize spatial locality, aligning data to cache line boundaries when practical, and minimizing random access patterns that cause frequent cache misses. Choosing appropriate buffer sizes based on workload and hardware characteristics is critical for balancing throughput and memory consumption.

Cache invalidation strategies should be carefully implemented based on application needs. For example, in data parallel computations, ex-

123

plicit synchronization points or atomic updates can ensure safe cache usage. Profiling tools assist in identifying cache miss rates and guiding optimization efforts.

Caching and buffering are instrumental techniques that significantly enhance system performance by reducing data access latency and smoothing data transfers. By understanding and applying principles of locality, choosing the right cache levels, and implementing efficient buffering, developers can create responsive, high-throughput applications well-suited to modern hardware architectures.

6

Input/Output and System Performance

This chapter examines how input/output operations influence overall system performance, highlighting their role as potential bottlenecks. It discusses various types of I/O, including file, network, and database interactions, and their distinct performance characteristics. Techniques for optimizing data transfer, such as batching and compression, are explained to improve efficiency. The chapter also introduces asynchronous and non-blocking I/O methods to reduce idle wait times and enhance throughput. Finally, it emphasizes the importance of measuring and diagnosing I/O bottlenecks using appropriate tools and techniques for targeted performance improvements.

6.1   How I/O Limits Program Speed

Input/output (I/O) operations represent a critical interface between a program and the external environment, encompassing activities such as reading or writing files on disk, sending or receiving data over a network, and interacting with user devices. In many software systems, I/O becomes the slowest portion of execution, often limiting the overall performance and responsiveness of a program. This section examines the characteristics that cause I/O operations to be bottlenecks, the consequences for system performance, and practical strategies to diagnose and mitigate such limitations.

The inherent nature of I/O operations distinguishes them sharply from internal CPU or memory activities. Whereas processors operate on the scale of nanoseconds to microseconds, and memory access commonly occurs within tens of nanoseconds, I/O operations involve comparatively slow subsystems. For example, mechanical hard drives require physical movement of read/write heads and rotational latency, while solid-state drives, although faster, still rely on complex electronics and communication protocols. Network communication introduces variability arising from transmission delays, routing, and signal propagation over sometimes large distances. Consequently, the latency and throughput associated with I/O are considerably lower than those achievable purely within the CPU and main memory.

Two fundamental metrics characterize I/O performance: latency and bandwidth. Latency is the time interval incurred before the beginning of data transfer after an I/O request is initiated. Bandwidth measures the maximum sustained rate of data transferred once the operation is underway. Table 6.1 contrasts typical latencies and bandwidths for var-

126

ious common I/O sources.

Table 6.1: *Typical latency and bandwidth for common I/O devices and interfaces*

I/O Device/Interface	Latency (microseconds)	Bandwidth (MB/s)
Mechanical Hard Drive (HDD)	5000–15000	80–160
Solid State Drive (SSD)	50–150	200–550
Network (Ethernet 1 Gbps)	50–100	125
Network (Wi-Fi 802.11ac)	100–300	200–600
USB 3.0 Flash Drive	100–300	100–400
RAM Memory Access	0.01	10000+
CPU L1 Cache Access	0.001	—

The table shows that even the fastest I/O devices generally have latency orders of magnitude higher than memory accesses. Bandwidth also tends to be constrained relative to the potential speeds of internal data transfers. These disparities fundamentally impact program execution when I/O operations must be completed before further processing proceeds.

During I/O operations, the CPU and program may enter a waiting state, pausing execution until the I/O device signals completion. Such *I/O wait times* produce idle CPU cycles and reduced resource utilization efficiency. In synchronous I/O models, the calling thread blocks during the entire I/O operation, magnifying this idle time. Even with modern multithreading, extensive blocking can constrain concurrency and reduce throughput. When a significant portion of total execution time is consumed by waiting for I/O completion, the program becomes *I/O bound*, meaning its speed is limited by the rate of I/O rather than computation.

This bottleneck effect has direct and measurable consequences on system performance. Programs bound by slow I/O will exhibit increased latency and decreased throughput, impairing responsiveness especially in interactive applications. It also complicates scaling, because adding additional CPU cores or faster processors does not proportionally enhance performance when the I/O subsystem remains a limiting factor. Performance tuning then requires addressing I/O inefficiencies to achieve meaningful improvement.

The following example output illustrates a hypothetical scenario where program execution time is dominated by disk read latency. The program attempts to process multiple data files sequentially, but waits for each disk read to complete before continuing calculation:

```
Starting data processing...
Reading file 1 of 10...
Read completed: 5.3 seconds
Processing data...
Reading file 2 of 10...
Read completed: 5.1 seconds
Processing data...
...
Total execution time: 65.4 seconds
Time spent waiting for disk I/O: 51.2 seconds
CPU processing time: 14.2 seconds
```

This output highlights that over 75% of the program's total runtime is attributed to waiting for slow disk operations, indicating a clear I/O bottleneck.

To identify and analyze such bottlenecks, various diagnostic tools can be employed. The iostat utility provides insight into device utilization, average queue length, and throughput of disk devices. Network analyzers like Wireshark capture packet-level data to determine network delay and packet loss. System monitoring tools track CPU usage along with I/O wait states, enabling determination of when and where performance degradation arises. Application-level logging and tracing can further pinpoint problematic I/O calls by recording timing and frequency statistics.

Once I/O bottlenecks are recognized, several optimization strategies become applicable.

- **Batching** aggregates multiple I/O operations into a single request to reduce per-operation overhead and increase effective throughput.

- **Caching** stores frequently accessed data in faster temporary storage to avoid repeated slow I/O fetches.

- **Asynchronous I/O** models allow programs to issue I/O requests without blocking, continuing computation or servicing other requests during wait periods. By overlapping I/O with computation or other tasks, asynchronous approaches reduce idle CPU time and enhance utilization.

The following code snippet demonstrates a simple batching technique using Python. Instead of writing each data item individually to disk, this approach collects multiple items in memory and writes them in bulk to reduce total I/O operations:

```python
def write_data_in_batches(filename, data, batch_size=1000):
    buffer = []
    with open(filename, 'w') as f:
        for item in data:
            buffer.append(item)
            if len(buffer) >= batch_size:
                f.write(''.join(buffer))
                buffer.clear()
        # Write any remaining items
        if buffer:
            f.write(''.join(buffer))

# Usage example
data_items = ['line {}\n'.format(i) for i in range(10000)]
```

```
write_data_in_batches('output.txt', data_items)
```

In this example, the `write_data_in_batches` function minimizes system calls by accumulating data before issuing the write operation, effectively reducing latency impacts and improving throughput.

In summary, the predominance of I/O latencies relative to processor and memory speeds causes I/O operations to frequently limit program performance. Understanding the characteristics of various I/O subsystems, diagnosing bottlenecks with appropriate tools, and applying mitigation strategies such as batching, caching, and asynchronous operations provide practical pathways to improved efficiency and responsiveness in software systems.

6.2 Types of I/O Operations

Input/output (I/O) operations form the essential interface through which programs interact with external systems and users. Understanding the distinct types of I/O and their performance characteristics is fundamental for designing efficient software. This section focuses on four primary categories of I/O: file system operations, network communication, database access, and user input. Each type exhibits unique performance profiles influenced by underlying hardware, software protocols, and user behavior, necessitating tailored approaches for optimization.

File I/O constitutes one of the most common interactions between a program and its environment. It involves reading from and writing to storage devices such as hard drives, solid-state drives, and network-attached storage. File I/O performance depends on device speed, file system efficiency, and operating system buffering mechanisms. Mechanical hard drives experience mechanical latency from moving parts, typically ranging in milliseconds, whereas solid-state drives present significantly reduced latency due to the absence of moving components. The throughput of file I/O is bounded by the device's maximum data transfer rate and the overhead in filesystem management, such as file allocation tables and caching strategies.

File I/O latency can adversely affect applications that perform frequent small reads or writes, where each operation incurs overhead. Conversely, sequential file access tends to achieve higher throughput due to prefetching and contiguous data layout. Operating systems often utilize write-back caches and read-ahead buffers to mitigate latency, but software design must also align with these mechanisms to maximize performance.

Network I/O introduces a fundamentally different set of performance considerations. It involves transmission of data packets across complex communication infrastructures, including wired and wireless networks, routers, switches, and firewalls. Network latency is influenced by propagation delays constrained by physical distance, transmission speed limits of communication channels, and additional processing delays at intermediate nodes. Unlike file I/O, network latency exhibits more variability and unpredictability, affected by congestion, packet loss, and retransmission delays.

Throughput in network communication depends on link bandwidth and protocol overheads, such as TCP/IP headers and error checking mechanisms. Wireless networks often feature fluctuating throughput caused by signal interference and environmental factors. Network operations also interact with security processes like encryption and tunneling, further influencing performance. Application-level protocols and connectivity stack implementations add layers of complexity affecting responsiveness.

Database I/O represents a specialized form of data interaction, combining aspects of file and network I/O but complicated by query processing, transaction management, and concurrency control. Database systems store large structured datasets and provide querying capabilities through languages such as SQL. Performance is contingent on multiple factors: indexing schemes optimize data retrieval paths, query complexity dictates computation time, and transaction overhead ensures atomicity and consistency.

Database I/O latency can vary substantially depending on query type—simple key-value lookups are fast when supported by indexes, while complex joins or aggregations require extensive computation and data access. Write operations incur additional costs from logging and locking mechanisms to maintain transactional integrity. Furthermore, multi-user environments introduce contention and potential bottlenecks due to concurrent access. The deployment architecture, whether centralized or distributed, also affects I/O timings due to network latency and replication delays.

User input I/O differs fundamentally from the other categories by involving human interaction or device-generated events such as keystrokes, mouse movements, or sensor signals. Its performance characteristics are inherently unpredictable because of user variability and hardware responsiveness. Processing user input demands efficient event handling to maintain application responsiveness. Delays in capturing, validating, and responding to input can impair user experience.

Signal processing hardware and drivers introduce latency, while software frameworks may buffer inputs or coalesce multiple events for efficiency. Strategies to handle user input efficiently often include debouncing, input validation to filter erroneous data early, and asynchronous event processing to decouple input handling from main application logic.

Table 6.2 summarizes key performance aspects of these I/O types, comparing typical latency ranges, bandwidth capabilities, frequent use cases, and associated trade-offs impacting optimization strategies.

Table 6.2: *Comparison of I/O Types: Latency, Bandwidth, Use Cases, and Trade-offs*

I/O Type	Latency	Bandwidth	Typical Use Cases	Performance Trade-offs
File I/O	Milliseconds (HDD), Microseconds (SSD)	Up to 550 MB/s (SSD)	Data storage, logs, config files	Small random access slower; buffering helps
Network I/O	Milliseconds to Seconds (variable)	100 Mbps to several Gbps	Web services, APIs, streaming	Variable latency; congestion impacts throughput
Database I/O	Milliseconds to Seconds	Depends on backend storage	Transactions, queries, analytics	Complexity of queries/key lookups; concurrency
User Input	Milliseconds to Seconds (user-dependent)	N/A (event-driven)	UI interaction, sensor inputs	Unpredictable timing; requires responsive handling

Efficient file access routines require careful design to minimize overhead and leverage operating system features. The code snippet below demonstrates basic file reading and writing in Python, emphasizing the use of buffered I/O to enhance performance. Buffered operations reduce the frequency of system calls by accumulating data in memory before transferring to storage.

```
# Writing data to a file with buffering
with open('data.txt', 'w', buffering=4096) as file:
    for i in range(1000):
        file.write(f'Line number {i}\n')

# Reading data from a file using buffering
with open('data.txt', 'r', buffering=4096) as file:
    for line in file:
        process(line)  # Placeholder for processing function
```

This example specifies a buffer size of 4096 bytes, a common page size for memory systems, to balance memory use and I/O efficiency. The underlying file system and operating system cache further improve performance by prefetching and delaying writes.

Network data transmission similarly benefits from structured interaction and buffering. The following code illustrates a simple TCP socket client and server model in Python using blocking calls for send and receive operations. It manifests underlying network latency and throughput constraints that influence program performance.

```
# Server code
import socket

server = socket.socket(socket.AF_INET, socket.SOCK_STREAM)
server.bind(('localhost', 8000))
server.listen(1)

conn, addr = server.accept()
with conn:
    while True:
        data = conn.recv(1024)
        if not data:
            break
        conn.sendall(data)  # Echo back

# Client code
import socket
```

```
client = socket.socket(socket.AF_INET, socket.SOCK_STREAM)
client.connect(('localhost', 8000))
client.sendall(b'Hello, world')
response = client.recv(1024)
print('Received:', response.decode())
client.close()
```

In this example, the size of data packets, network delays, and socket buffering impact the speed and responsiveness of both endpoints. Careful tuning of buffer sizes, message framing, and connection management can optimize performance depending on application needs.

Database I/O involves interaction between application software and database management systems (DBMS). When an application submits a query, the DBMS parses and plans execution, accessing stored data through indexes or scanning tables. Disk access and cache hits determine physical I/O costs. Network latency is incurred when databases reside on remote servers. Transactions with locking and concurrency control add overheads, and query optimization seeks to minimize redundant reads or expensive joins.

Efficient database interaction techniques include indexing crucial fields used in queries, batching multiple operations within transactions to reduce round trips, and caching query results to prevent repeated expensive I/O. Proper schema design and workload analysis enhance data retrieval times and consistency without sacrificing performance.

User input processing represents a domain requiring responsiveness above raw throughput. Typical sources include keyboards, mice, touchscreens, and specialized sensors. Input event handling frameworks buffer input events and dispatch them asynchronously to application handlers. Latencies derive from device polling rates, driver stack processing, and system load. Unpredictability is inherent as user pace and behavior vary.

To manage these challenges, software employs input validation to discard erroneous or unexpected data promptly. Debouncing techniques ensure multiple rapid signals are interpreted correctly, avoiding redundant processing. Asynchronous event-driven models allow input handling without blocking other program parts, maintaining user interface fluidity and reducing perceptible delays.

This section has outlined the distinguishing characteristics and performance implications of major I/O types. A pragmatic understanding of these differences enables developers to make informed choices in the design of I/O handling, improving overall software efficiency and user experience.

6.3 Optimizing Data Transfer

Efficient data transfer is essential for improving the performance of programs that rely heavily on input/output operations. Techniques such as batching, data aggregation, and compression are fundamental for reducing the time and resources needed to move data between components, devices, or networks. These methods help minimize latency, maximize throughput, and leverage available system capabilities, ultimately mitigating bottlenecks in I/O-bound applications.

Batching groups multiple data items or requests into a single operation. Rather than sending or processing many small units, batching reduces overhead by amortizing fixed costs such as system call invocation, protocol handshake, or device initialization over larger payloads. This reduction in the number of discrete operations decreases waiting times, increases utilization of hardware buffers, and enhances through-put. For example, instead of writing individual records to disk one at a time, an application can accumulate many records in memory and write them in fewer, larger blocks.

Data aggregation combines data across multiple sources, time inter-vals, or dimensions before transmission. Aggregation lowers the fre-quency of transfers and decreases the volume of redundant or less relevant data sent. By consolidating information, systems reduce net-work congestion, disk I/O pressure, and downstream processing cost. Aggregated data may represent averages, sums, or other summaries depending on application requirements. This method is especially ef-fective in sensor networks, distributed logging, and analytic workloads where periodic reporting of summarized data suffices and continuous raw data streaming is unnecessary.

Compression reduces the size of data to be transferred by encoding in-formation more succinctly. This method lowers bandwidth needs and shortens transfer durations. The trade-off lies in the computational cost to compress and decompress data, consuming CPU cycles and potentially introducing latency. Compression algorithms vary widely in speed and compression ratio, allowing selection tailored to specific system constraints. Lossless compression techniques ensure complete data integrity, which is vital for critical applications; in contrast, lossy compression may be acceptable in multimedia contexts where some fidelity loss is tolerable.

Combining compression with batching and aggregation can yield mul-tiplicative gains. Large batches of aggregated data often compress more effectively than small, fragmented datasets due to redundancy and repeating patterns at scale. For instance, textual logs batched to-gether typically yield higher compression ratios than isolated lines.

Moreover, carefully designed workflows synchronize batching intervals with compression schedules to optimally balance latency and resource efficiency.

The following Python code snippet illustrates batching for network data transmission. This example accumulates multiple messages in a buffer and sends them together, thereby reducing the number of send operations and associated overhead:

```python
import socket

def send_batch(sock, messages, batch_size=10):
    buffer = []
    for msg in messages:
        buffer.append(msg)
        if len(buffer) >= batch_size:
            data = ''.join(buffer).encode('utf-8')
            sock.sendall(data)
            buffer.clear()
    # Send any remaining messages
    if buffer:
        data = ''.join(buffer).encode('utf-8')
        sock.sendall(data)

# Example usage
sock = socket.socket(socket.AF_INET, socket.SOCK_STREAM)
sock.connect(('example.com', 12345))

messages = [f"message {i}\n" for i in range(100)]
send_batch(sock, messages)
sock.close()
```

In this example, messages are concatenated and sent in groups of ten, reducing the number of system calls and making network communication more efficient. The choice of batch size depends on factors such as network MTU, latency sensitivity, and memory constraints.

To demonstrate data compression, consider the following Python snippet using the gzip module. It compresses a string prior to transmission

138

and then decompresses it on the receiver side:

```
import gzip

def compress_data(data):
    return gzip.compress(data.encode('utf-8'))

def decompress_data(compressed_data):
    return gzip.decompress(compressed_data).decode('utf-8')

# Example usage
original_data = "This is some example text that will be compressed."
compressed = compress_data(original_data)
print(f"Original size: {len(original_data)} bytes")
print(f"Compressed size: {len(compressed)} bytes")

decompressed = decompress_data(compressed)
print(f"Decompressed data: {decompressed}")
```

This code shows how compression reduces the size of textual data before sending while ensuring that the original content can be fully restored. Compression is particularly effective for repetitive or verbose data, such as logs, configuration files, or large JSON responses.

While batching and compression improve data transfer performance, they involve trade-offs. Batching increases latency because data accumulates before transmission; overly large batches delay delivery and reduce interactivity for latency-sensitive applications. Conversely, too small batches may not amortize overhead effectively. Compression lowers bandwidth usage but adds CPU overhead; excessive compression workloads can offset latency gains, especially on resource-constrained devices. Selecting an optimal combination requires profiling and balancing system priorities.

The following figure conceptually demonstrates transfer time before and after applying batching and compression optimizations. The horizontal axis represents data size, and the vertical axis shows time in milliseconds. The unoptimized line rises steeply as data size increases, reflecting frequent small transmissions. The batching-only line displays improved scaling with larger, fewer transmissions. The combined batching and compression line further reduces transfer times substantially, especially for larger datasets with compressible content.

```
Transfer Time vs. Data Size

Time (ms)

  Unoptimized
   /
   /
   /
  Batching /
  -------/
   /
  Combined Batching + Compression
  ____/ _____ Data Size
```

Figure 6.1: *Conceptual illustration of transfer time as a function of data size under different optimization strategies.*

Empirical observations emphasize the importance of correctly choosing batch sizes to minimize latency without incurring excessive memory consumption. Similarly, the selection of a compression algorithm depends on the data type and available CPU capacity. For example, fast algorithms like LZ4 offer moderate compression with minimal CPU load, while modules that achieve higher compression ratios may require more CPU cycles.

Best practices recommend profiling the specific application workload to identify bottlenecks and fine-tune parameters accordingly. Batching should be aligned with application semantics; for real-time systems, small batches or even no batching might be preferable, whereas large-scale data processing favors larger batches. Compression decisions require considering network bandwidth, CPU cycles, and acceptable latency.

Additionally, combining batching and compression may necessitate adjustments to error handling and retransmission strategies to account for the larger atomic units of transfer. Testing under realistic workloads ensures that performance gains are achieved without compromising correctness or user experience.

By applying these techniques thoughtfully, engineers can significantly enhance the efficiency of data movement, alleviating common I/O bottlenecks and improving overall system responsiveness.

6.4 Asynchronous and Non-blocking I/O

Traditional input/output operations often require programs to wait for completion before proceeding, resulting in idle CPU time and reduced throughput. Asynchronous and non-blocking I/O techniques present an alternative approach that allows programs to initiate I/O operations without halting execution. This event-driven methodology enables more efficient use of system resources by overlapping computation and data transfers, ultimately reducing latency and improving scalability.

Asynchronous I/O (AIO) encompasses programming models where an I/O request returns immediately, permitting the initiating process to continue performing other tasks. Completion of the I/O is typically signaled later via callbacks, events, or future-promises, allowing the program to react to data availability or operation conclusion without blocking. Unlike synchronous blocking I/O, AIO decouples request initiation and result handling, enabling high concurrency and responsiveness particularly in I/O-bound workloads involving multiple simultaneous operations.

The event-driven programming model forms the conceptual foundation of asynchronous I/O. In this paradigm, the program flow is determined by external or internal events such as data arrival, timer expirations, or user actions. Instead of executing sequentially and waiting for each blocking I/O call to finish, the application registers event handlers or callback functions that the system invokes when corresponding events occur. This setup demands a fundamentally different design from traditional procedural code, emphasizing modular, reactive components that process events as they happen.

Non-blocking I/O mechanisms implement this model at the system-call level, allowing I/O operations to be initiated without suspending the calling thread. APIs such as `select`, `poll`, and `epoll` on Unix-like systems, or `IOCP` on Windows, allow programs to monitor multiple I/O descriptors and respond only when data or readiness signals are available. These APIs return immediately from calls that would typically block, enabling the application to multiplex I/O on a single thread or across multiple threads efficiently.

Consider the following Python example demonstrating asynchronous file reading using the `asyncio` library. The code uses `aiofiles` to perform non-blocking file operations with `await` expressions that suspend the coroutine only while waiting for actual I/O events, instead of blocking the entire thread:

```
import asyncio
import aiofiles

async def read_file_async(filename):
    async with aiofiles.open(filename, 'r') as f:
```

```
      contents = await f.read()
    return contents

async def main():
    data = await read_file_async('example.txt')
    print(data)

asyncio.run(main())
```

This example illustrates how asynchronous file I/O frees the event loop to execute other tasks or handle additional I/O while waiting for the file read operation to complete, rather than blocking execution.

Central to asynchronous I/O systems is the *event loop*, a control structure that manages and dispatches events and callbacks. The event loop continually monitors subscribed I/O sources, timers, and signals, invoking the appropriate event handlers when events occur. It acts as the coordinator that allows a single thread or process to efficiently manage multiple concurrent asynchronous operations by sequentially invoking ready callbacks and re-entering a wait state otherwise.

Handling multiple I/O events efficiently within this model requires careful design. The program maintains a queue or set of pending operations and their associated callbacks or futures. When the underlying system signals readiness, the event loop dispatches corresponding handlers, which may in turn initiate further asynchronous operations. This chaining creates a flow of event-driven processing without blocking any individual step. Cooperative multitasking frameworks augment this model, enabling coroutines to yield control explicitly to maintain responsiveness.

Asynchronous I/O improves resource utilization by reducing idle CPU time traditionally spent waiting on slow I/O subsystems. It increases throughput by allowing more simultaneous operations within the same process or thread context. This approach reduces context-switch overhead associated with multithreading and better scales under high concurrency, as seen in modern servers, networked applications, and user interface frameworks.

The next example portrays a non-blocking network request implemented using Python's `asyncio` and `aiohttp` libraries. This pattern illustrates concurrent network communication without blocking the main execution flow:

```python
import asyncio
import aiohttp

async def fetch_url(session, url):
    async with session.get(url) as response:
        return await response.text()

async def main():
    async with aiohttp.ClientSession() as session:
        urls = [
            'https://example.com',
            'https://python.org',
            'https://github.com'
        ]
        tasks = [fetch_url(session, url) for url in urls]
        responses = await asyncio.gather(*tasks)
        for content in responses:
            print('Received {} bytes'.format(len(content)))

asyncio.run(main())
```

Here, multiple HTTP GET requests proceed concurrently. The event loop interleaves their operations and calls back as data arrives, preventing thread blocking and maximizing network utilization.

The workflow of asynchronous I/O can be visualized as follows, showing how the event loop manages multiple outstanding I/O operations and their respective callbacks:

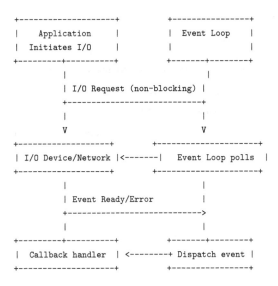

```
+--------------------+          +----------------+
|    Application     |          |  Event Loop    |
|   Initiates I/O    |          |                |
+---------+----------+          +-------+--------+
          |                             |
          | I/O Request (non-blocking)  |
          +---------------------------+
          |                             |
          V                             V
+--------------------+          +----------------------+
| I/O Device/Network |<-------|    Event Loop polls    |
+--------------------+          +----------------------+
          |                             |
          | Event Ready/Error           |
          +--------------------------->
          |                             |
+---------+----------+          +-------+--------+
|  Callback handler  | <--------+ Dispatch event |
+--------------------+          +----------------+
```

The event loop pattern exemplifies how asynchronous I/O frameworks maintain program responsiveness while managing multiple concurrent I/O sources on minimal threads.

To design maintainable, efficient, and reliable asynchronous I/O systems, several best practices are recommended. Clear separation of event handler logic promotes modularity and ease of understanding. Avoidance of blocking calls inside asynchronous contexts is critical to prevent stalling the event loop. Proper error handling inside callbacks ensures robustness under I/O failures. Resource cleanup, such as closing file descriptors and cancelling pending tasks, prevents leaks. Using high-level abstractions like futures or promises simplifies asynchronous flow control and reduces callback nesting.

Furthermore, profiling and monitoring should target asynchronous workloads, as concurrency adds complexity to identifying bottlenecks. Testing asynchronous code requires care with timing and ordering of events. Documentation should specify expected execution patterns and lifecycle of asynchronous operations.

Adopting asynchronous and non-blocking I/O harnesses system capabilities far beyond what traditional synchronous models can achieve. It is particularly effective in applications requiring high concurrency, low latency, and optimal utilization of CPU and I/O resources. Mastery of these techniques enables developers to build scalable, responsive, and efficient software systems in an increasingly interconnected and multitasking computing landscape.

6.5   Measuring and Debugging I/O Bottlenecks

Understanding and improving the performance of software systems requires precise identification of bottlenecks, especially those caused by input/output (I/O) operations. I/O bottlenecks often lead to excessive waiting, poor responsiveness, and degraded throughput. Detecting these problems early through measurement and analysis is key to targeted optimization efforts, avoiding wasted resources and ineffective tuning.

Measuring I/O performance involves collecting metrics such as latency, throughput, utilization, and wait times for different I/O devices and interfaces. Profiling tools provide invaluable assistance in gathering this data, offering insights into where delays occur, how resources are consumed, and which operations dominate execution time. These tools vary in granularity and scope, addressing disk I/O, network packets, system-wide monitoring, or application-specific tracing.

Table 8.2 summarizes several popular I/O profiling tools, describing their primary use cases and distinguishing features.

146

Table 6.3: *Comparison of Popular I/O Profiling Tools*

Tool	Primary Use	Key Features
iostat	Disk I/O statistics	Device utilization, throughput, I/O wait times
dstat	System-wide resource monitoring	CPU, disk, network, memory, customizable reports
Wireshark	Network traffic analysis	Packet capture, protocol decoding, filtering
perf	Performance profiling	CPU, I/O events, sampling-based analysis
System monitors (top, htop)	Process and resource overview	Real-time CPU, memory, disk I/O per process

Collecting system metrics during program execution grants visibility into how I/O operations affect performance. Metrics such as I/O wait time quantify the fraction of CPU cycles spent waiting for I/O completion, revealing whether the processor is idle due to slow devices. Throughput (bytes per second) indicates data transfer efficiency, while latency measures how long individual operations take from request to completion. Combining these data points enables diagnosis of whether delays arise from device saturation, inefficient access patterns, or software-level issues.

Detailed logging and tracing augment statistical metrics by capturing temporal sequences and contextual information about I/O events. System call tracing tools or application instrumentation can record timestamps, call stacks, and parameters for I/O requests. Analyzing these logs facilitates detection of repeated delays, hotspots of intensive I/O, or unexpected behavior like partial reads and retries. Tracing is especially useful when profiling overhead must be minimal or when debugging complex multi-threaded or distributed systems.

The following command demonstrates the use of the iostat tool to monitor disk I/O statistics over a five-second interval with two-second

147

updates. It captures utilization, read/write throughput, and request rates for each block device:

```
iostat -x 2 5
```

This command outputs extended statistics every two seconds for five cycles, enabling real-time observation of device load and identifying periods of saturation or queuing.

Interpreting profiling data requires understanding the meaning of collected metrics and identifying patterns indicative of bottlenecks. High device utilization (near 100%) suggests saturation where requests queue and wait times increase. Elevated I/O wait times on the CPU indicate that processes are stalled waiting for I/O completion, often accompanied by low CPU utilization. Disproportionately high latency for particular request types or devices signals inefficient access or hardware problems. Consistent throughput below expected device capacities points to software or configuration limitations.

Consider the following example output from monitoring a storage device before and after remediation of an I/O bottleneck:

```
Before optimization:
Device     %util  await  r/sec  w/sec
sda        98.5   25.7   500    450

After optimization:
Device     %util  await  r/sec  w/sec
sda        65.2   9.3    600    700
```

The initial state exhibits very high utilization and average wait times of 25.7 ms, indicating a bottleneck. After optimizing I/O access patterns and introducing batching, device utilization and latency decrease while throughput increases, resulting in better performance.

148

Common causes of I/O bottlenecks include hardware limitations such as disk or network saturation, fragmentation, or faulty devices. Software issues arise from inefficient algorithms, excessive small I/O operations, lock contention in multi-threaded environments, or poor caching strategies. Network bottlenecks may result from bandwidth constraints, latency spikes due to congestion, or protocol inefficiencies. Recognizing these patterns guides developers toward appropriate mitigations.

Effective strategies to alleviate I/O bottlenecks include caching frequently accessed data in memory to reduce repeated device access, batching operations to amortize overhead, and load balancing across multiple resources to prevent hotspots. Optimizing access patterns by aligning requests with device layouts or employing asynchronous I/O can minimize wait times. Network optimizations may involve tuning buffer sizes, compressing data, or prioritizing critical traffic.

A systematic workflow for I/O diagnostics helps consistently identify and resolve performance issues. The following pseudocode outlines a typical process:

```
procedure Diagnose_IO_Bottleneck()
    start_system_monitoring()
    run_target_application()
    collect_IO_metrics()
    if IO_utilization_high() or IO_wait_time_high() then
        identify_heavy_IO_operations()
        analyze_access_patterns()
        check_hardware_status()
        apply_optimizations()  // e.g., caching, batching
        rerun_tests()
        if performance_improved() then
            document_changes()
        else
            escalate_to_detailed_tracing()
    else
        confirm_IO_not_bottleneck()
```

```
      end if
end procedure
```

This approach emphasizes iterative testing, metric-driven analysis, and progressive refinement of the system. By monitoring initial conditions, isolating problematic I/O components, and applying informed optimizations, developers can systematically improve application performance.

Measuring and debugging I/O bottlenecks demand a combination of monitoring tools, careful interpretation of metrics, detailed logging, and iterative refinement. Comprehensive profiling uncovers critical inefficiencies, while targeted diagnostics support effective optimizations. Employing these techniques ensures that I/O operations do not unduly hinder system responsiveness or throughput.

7

Concurrency, Parallelism, and Hardware Awareness

This chapter discusses the fundamental concepts of concurrency and parallelism, highlighting their differences, benefits, and appropriate use cases. It explains process, thread, and task models, emphasizing how they influence performance and resource utilization. The chapter addresses common pitfalls such as race conditions, deadlocks, and synchronization issues, providing strategies to avoid them. It also explores modern hardware features like multicore processors, cache hierarchies, and SIMD instructions, illustrating their role in enhancing performance. Finally, it reviews techniques and tools for designing scalable, hardware-aware software that efficiently exploits available system resources.

7.1 Concurrency vs. Parallelism

In the domain of modern software development, understanding the distinction between concurrency and parallelism is essential for designing efficient programs that maximize resource utilization and meet performance objectives. These concepts, while related, address different challenges and offer unique benefits depending on the nature of the tasks and the underlying hardware.

Concurrency refers to the management of multiple tasks that make progress during overlapping time periods. It does not necessarily imply that these tasks are executing simultaneously at the exact instant; rather, concurrency allows a system to handle many tasks by interleaving their execution, often through mechanisms such as multitasking, context switching, or asynchronous programming. This enables a single processing unit to switch between tasks rapidly enough that the user or system observes progress in all tasks concurrently.

Parallelism, on the other hand, denotes the simultaneous execution of multiple tasks. It requires multiple processing units—such as multiple cores or processors—to literally perform different computations at the same time. Parallelism can dramatically reduce the total elapsed time for compute-intensive tasks by dividing the workload among available processors, enabling true simultaneous data processing and computation.

To clarify the distinctions between these two concepts, the following table summarizes their core characteristics, benefits, and typical application domains:

Concurrency improves a program's ability to handle multiple operations in overlapping time frames, which is especially valuable in I/O-

Aspect	Concurrency	Parallelism
Definition	Overlapping execution of tasks through interleaving or asynchronous operations	Simultaneous execution of multiple tasks on multiple processors or cores
Underlying Hardware	Can be implemented on a single processor using time-slicing or asynchronous I/O	Requires multiple processors or cores for true simultaneous execution
Goal	Efficient resource utilization and improved responsiveness	Reduced total computation time for intensive workloads
Typical Use Cases	I/O-bound applications, user interface responsiveness, event-driven systems	CPU-bound batch processing, scientific computations, large-scale data processing
Complexity	High synchronization complexity due to shared resource management	Complexity in workload partitioning and coordination among processing units
Performance Impact	Improves throughput and responsiveness, especially when tasks are waiting for external events	Offers speedup proportional to the number of available processors for parallelizable tasks

Table 7.1: *Comparison between concurrency and parallelism*

bound and interactive applications. For instance, a web server managing several simultaneous user requests benefits from concurrency by initiating multiple input or output operations without blocking the entire system while waiting for each operation to complete. This approach maximizes resource utilization, since while one task waits for I/O completion, the processor can work on other tasks rather than remaining idle. Additionally, concurrent designs enhance responsiveness, providing timely feedback to users or external systems even when the overall workload is high.

Parallelism delivers acceleration by dividing computing tasks into independent units of work that run in true simultaneous fashion across multiple CPU cores or processors. This model is well-suited for CPU-intensive problems, including matrix operations, large-scale simula-

153

tions, data analytics, and machine learning tasks. By leveraging parallel hardware, such workloads can achieve substantial reductions in total execution time, often approximately dividing the time by the number of processing units used (subject to task dependencies and communication overhead). Effective parallelization depends on the ability
to partition work into discrete chunks that can be processed independently or with minimal synchronization.

Determining when to use concurrency or parallelism depends largely
on the workload characteristics and the performance goals of the program. Concurrency is particularly advantageous when the application
involves multiple I/O operations or event-driven tasks that spend time
waiting for external devices, network responses, or user input. This
allows the system to remain productive and responsive by switching
between tasks rather than idling during waits. For example, network
servers, graphical user interfaces, and real-time monitoring systems
commonly use concurrency to maintain responsiveness under load.

Conversely, parallelism is the preferred strategy when the primary
goal is to accelerate compute-bound work, where the tasks are processor intensive, have minimal interdependencies, and can be decom-
posed into parallel subtasks. Examples include compressing large
media files, performing mathematical simulations, or processing big
data. Parallel implementations harness multiple CPU cores to execute
these computations simultaneously, substantially shortening processing times compared to sequential execution.

To illustrate concurrency, consider a program written in a language
supporting asynchronous programming or multithreading that reads
data from multiple files and processes them concurrently without
blocking on each file read. The example below in Python demonstrates
concurrent reading using threads:

```
import threading

def read_file(filename):
    with open(filename, 'r') as f:
        data = f.read()
        print(f"Read {len(data)} characters from {filename}")

files = ['file1.txt', 'file2.txt', 'file3.txt']
threads = []

for file in files:
    thread = threading.Thread(target=read_file, args=(file,))
    threads.append(thread)
    thread.start()

for thread in threads:
    thread.join()
```

In this example, each file is read in a separate thread, allowing multiple I/O-bound reading operations to overlap. While one thread waits for disk I/O, others may continue execution or manage different files, improving overall throughput.

For parallelism, consider a computationally intensive operation like matrix multiplication. The following example, written in C++ with OpenMP directives, illustrates parallel processing by distributing the multiplication work over multiple CPU cores:

```
#include <omp.h>
void matmul(const double* A, const double* B, double* C, int N) {
    #pragma omp parallel for collapse(2)
    for (int i = 0; i < N; ++i) {
        for (int j = 0; j < N; ++j) {
            double sum = 0.0;
            for (int k = 0; k < N; ++k) {
                sum += A[i * N + k] * B[k * N + j];
            }
            C[i * N + j] = sum;
        }
    }
}
```

```
}
```

The #pragma omp parallel for directive instructs the compiler to run the nested loops concurrently across available processor cores, accelerating the entire matrix multiplication task.

Performance comparisons between concurrent and parallel implementations typically reveal distinct trade-offs in resource usage and latency. Concurrent programs efficiently manage resources and improve responsiveness but may not significantly reduce total computation time for CPU-heavy tasks. Parallel programs achieve speedup proportional to processor count but can incur overhead from synchronization and data sharing. The graph below conceptually illustrates that concurrency improves responsiveness but achieves limited speedup in CPU tasks, while parallelism yields substantial speedup for compute-heavy workloads:

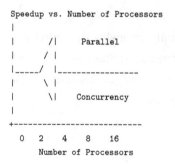

```
Speedup vs. Number of Processors
|
|       /|      Parallel
|      / |
|_____/  |_____
|     \  |
|      \|       Concurrency
|
+---------------------------
  0   2   4   8   16
      Number of Processors
```

Choosing between concurrency and parallelism requires careful consideration of hardware capabilities, workload patterns, and performance objectives. If the execution environment has a single processor or the tasks are primarily I/O-bound or event-driven, concurrency yields better system responsiveness and resource use. If multiple pro-

156

cessors or cores are available and the tasks are compute-bound with parallelizable workloads, parallelism should be preferred to leverage hardware for acceleration.

In some cases, combining both techniques provides a comprehensive solution. A system may use concurrency to handle multiple I/O operations and user interactions while employing parallelism to speed up internal computations when processor capacity allows. Understanding the nature of the workload, external resource dependencies, and hardware is fundamental to selecting the appropriate model to maximize program efficiency and responsiveness.

7.2 Processes, Threads, and Tasks

In software execution, the concepts of processes, threads, and tasks are fundamental for understanding how programs utilize system resources and achieve efficient execution. Each of these abstractions represents a different level of execution and resource management, significantly impacting program design and performance.

A *process* is an instance of a running program, which has its own isolated memory space, system resources such as file descriptors, and execution context including program counters and registers. Processes operate independently, with each process running in its own virtual address space. This isolation provides robustness and security, as processes cannot directly interfere with each other's memory or resources without explicit inter-process communication. When a program is executed, the operating system creates a process to manage its execution.

Threads are subdivisions of processes and represent smaller units of execution that share the same memory space and resources within

157

a process. Each thread maintains its own execution context, including its own program counter, stack, and registers, but accesses shared data and code in the process's memory. Threads are also known as lightweight processes because they provide concurrent execution within a single process with significantly lower overhead compared to multiple processes. Multiple threads within a process can execute different parts of the program simultaneously or concurrently, enabling efficient use of CPU resources.

The differences between processes and threads extend beyond their memory and resource models to their performance characteristics, such as creation overhead, context switching costs, and communication complexity. To clarify, the following table compares essential performance attributes of processes and threads:

Characteristic	Processes	Threads
Memory and Resource Ownership	Own separate memory space and system resources	Share memory and system resources within the process
Creation Overhead	Higher due to allocating separate memory and resources	Lower, since threads share existing process resources
Context Switching Cost	Relatively high due to switching entire process context	Lower, as only thread-specific context is switched
Communication	Requires inter-process communication (IPC) mechanisms (e.g., pipes, sockets)	Can communicate directly through shared memory
Fault Isolation	Faults typically limited to one process	Faults in one thread may affect entire process

Table 7.2: *Performance characteristics comparison between processes and threads*

The *task* model abstracts a schedulable unit of work that can be managed either by threads or processes. Tasks represent logical units of computation or jobs that the scheduler handles to utilize the CPU effectively. Tasks may vary in complexity and execution time, and they serve as the basis for parallel and concurrent program architectures.

158

By scheduling tasks to available threads or processes, the system can flexibly balance workloads and optimize resource utilization.

An example of creating a process in a UNIX-like operating system is demonstrated by the usage of the fork() system call in C, which creates a new child process as a copy of the parent:

```c
#include <unistd.h>
#include <stdio.h>

int main() {
    pid_t pid = fork();

    if (pid == -1) {
        // Fork failed
        perror("fork");
        return 1;
    } else if (pid == 0) {
        // Child process
        printf("This is the child process.\n");
    } else {
        // Parent process
        printf("This is the parent process, child PID is %d.\n", pid);
    }

    return 0;
}
```

This code demonstrates creation of a new process that runs concurrently with the parent process, allowing the operating system to schedule both independently.

In contrast, creating a thread within a program can be done using threading libraries such as POSIX threads (pthreads) in C. The following example creates a thread that executes a simple function and demonstrates basic synchronization using a mutex to protect shared data:

```c
#include <pthread.h>
```

```
#include <stdio.h>

int shared_counter = 0;
pthread_mutex_t lock;

void* increment(void* arg) {
    pthread_mutex_lock(&lock);
    shared_counter++;
    printf("Counter: %d\n", shared_counter);
    pthread_mutex_unlock(&lock);
    return NULL;
}

int main() {
    pthread_t thread;
    pthread_mutex_init(&lock, NULL);

    pthread_create(&thread, NULL, increment, NULL);
    pthread_join(thread, NULL);

    pthread_mutex_destroy(&lock);
    return 0;
}
```

This example illustrates the low overhead of thread creation compared to process creation, and how synchronization primitives such as mutexes are essential to coordinate access to shared data and avoid race conditions.

The choice between using processes or threads influences performance characteristics significantly. Thread creation typically involves less overhead in both time and memory than process creation, mainly because threads share many of the parent's resources. Likewise, context switches between threads are often faster than between processes, as the operating system does not need to switch memory mappings or flush caches entirely. However, threads also increase the risk of concurrency bugs such as data races and deadlocks, since they share the same address space. Processes provide stronger isolation, reducing interferences and potential corruption from other concurrently executing tasks.

Synchronization and inter-task communication are additional critical considerations in multithreaded and multiprocess applications. Synchronization mechanisms such as mutexes, semaphores, condition variables, and barriers allow coordinated access to shared resources and prevent inconsistent states. Message passing provides a safe communication method between processes without shared memory, often implemented via pipes, sockets, or other IPC methods.

The following summarizes common synchronization primitives and their use cases:

- **Mutexes** (mutual exclusion locks) enforce exclusive access to critical sections of code or shared data.

- **Semaphores** regulate access to a limited number of resources by maintaining a count of available units.

- **Condition variables** allow threads to wait for certain conditions or events to occur.

- **Barriers** synchronize threads at a point so all must arrive before continuing.

- **Message Passing** facilitates communication in a process-isolated manner without shared memory, reducing synchronization complexity.

Efficient task scheduling plays a vital role in performance and responsiveness of concurrent programs. Several scheduling algorithms influence how threads or processes receive CPU time, affecting latency, fairness, and throughput. Key scheduling policies include:

161

Scheduling Algorithm	Description	Performance Impacts
Round-Robin	Assigns fixed time slices to each task in cyclic order	Simple, fair sharing; good for interactive systems but can increase context switching overhead
Priority-Based	Tasks are scheduled based on assigned priorities	Enables critical tasks to execute sooner but risks starvation of low-priority tasks
Multilevel Queue	Tasks categorized in queues with different priorities; separate scheduling in each queue	Balances priorities and fairness; useful for heterogeneous workloads
Fair-Share	Allocates CPU time based on user or group quotas	Ensures equitable resource distribution across users

Table 7.3: *Common task scheduling algorithms and their performance considerations*

Choosing an appropriate scheduling strategy depends on workload requirements, responsiveness goals, and real-time constraints. For example, interactive applications benefit from round-robin schedules with short time slices to maintain responsiveness, whereas batch processing tasks may tolerate longer slices or priority scheduling to maximize throughput.

Balancing process and thread utilization, selecting appropriate synchronization mechanisms, and deploying an effective scheduling strategy are essential for designing software systems that meet specific performance goals while maintaining stability and safety. Understanding these fundamental models and their implications equips programmers to exploit hardware capabilities effectively and construct robust concurrent applications.

7.3 Avoiding Common Pitfalls

Concurrent programming introduces complexity that can lead to subtle and difficult-to-diagnose issues. Among the most frequent problems encountered are race conditions, deadlocks, and synchronization errors. These issues arise when multiple threads or processes interact without appropriate coordination, resulting in unpredictable behavior, application freezes, or degraded performance. Developing a clear understanding of these pitfalls and employing strategies to avoid them is fundamental for writing robust and efficient concurrent software.

A *race condition* occurs when two or more concurrent tasks access shared data simultaneously, and at least one of the accesses involves modification. Without proper synchronization, the order of execution between these tasks is non-deterministic, leading to inconsistent or corrupted data states. Since modern processors execute instructions and threads in parallel or interleaved fashion, even a seemingly straightforward program can exhibit intermittent and non-reproducible errors due to race conditions.

Deadlocks represent another critical concurrency problem where two or more tasks become stuck indefinitely, each waiting for resources that the other holds. This circular dependency creates a situation in which none of the tasks can proceed, effectively halting parts of the program. Deadlocks are often caused by improper ordering of locks or resource acquisitions, and once a deadlock occurs, it typically requires external intervention to resolve.

Synchronization issues extend beyond race conditions and deadlocks, encompassing problems like excessive locking leading to performance bottlenecks, or inconsistent use of locking that causes livelocks or starvation. Incorrect or overly coarse locking granularity can degrade the responsiveness and throughput of the system, while improper lock usage can introduce new concurrency bugs.

An exemplary illustration of a race condition is shown in the following Python snippet, where two threads increment a shared counter without synchronization:

```
import threading

counter = 0

def increment():
    global counter
    for _ in range(100000):
        counter += 1

thread1 = threading.Thread(target=increment)
thread2 = threading.Thread(target=increment)
thread1.start()
thread2.start()
thread1.join()
thread2.join()

print(f"Final counter value: {counter}")
```

This program may produce a final counter value less than the expected 200,000 because the increment operation is not atomic; the threads may read, modify, and write the counter concurrently, overwriting each other's updates.

To resolve this, we introduce a lock to ensure mutual exclusion during the increment:

```
import threading

counter = 0
lock = threading.Lock()
```

```
def increment():
    global counter
    for _ in range(100000):
        with lock:
            counter += 1

thread1 = threading.Thread(target=increment)
thread2 = threading.Thread(target=increment)
thread1.start()
thread2.start()
thread1.join()
thread2.join()

print(f"Final counter value: {counter}")
```

By acquiring the lock before modifying the counter, the threads enforce exclusive access, preventing interleaved updates and ensuring the final value is as expected.

Deadlocks can be demonstrated using the following C-like pseudocode where two threads attempt to acquire two locks in opposite order:

```
lock1.acquire()
lock2.acquire()
// Critical section
lock2.release()
lock1.release()

// Meanwhile, in another thread:
lock2.acquire()
lock1.acquire()
// Critical section
lock1.release()
lock2.release()
```

If the first thread acquires lock1 and waits for lock2 while the second thread holds lock2 and waits for lock1, both threads block indefinitely, resulting in a deadlock.

165

Several strategies are effective in preventing race conditions. Employing mutual exclusion locks ensures that critical sections that access shared data are executed by only one thread at a time. For finer granularity and potential performance gains, atomic operations—provided by modern processor instruction sets or language libraries—allow specific memory updates to be performed indivisibly without locks. Design patterns like immutable data structures or message passing architectures can reduce shared mutable state, minimizing the risk of race conditions.

Deadlocks can be mitigated by enforcing a strict global ordering on resource acquisition. By ensuring all threads acquire locks in the same predetermined order, circular wait conditions cannot arise. Additionally, the use of timeout mechanisms when obtaining locks can prevent indefinite blocking, allowing threads to back off and retry. Some systems implement deadlock detection algorithms that monitor resource dependencies and resolve deadlocks dynamically, although this approach is more complex.

Effective synchronization balances safety with performance. Overuse of locks may serialize program execution, eliminating parallelism and increasing contention. Conversely, insufficient synchronization leads to unpredictable behavior. Best practices include minimizing the scope and duration of critical sections, using finer-grained locks when possible, favoring lock-free algorithms and atomics when appropriate, and avoiding unnecessary sharing of mutable state. Thorough code reviews and testing focusing on concurrent scenarios help detect synchronization issues early.

Race Condition Example:
Thread A: Read shared_var
Thread B: Read shared_var
Thread A: shared_var = shared_var + 1
Thread B: shared_var = shared_var + 1
Result: One increment lost due to interleaving

Deadlock Example:
Thread A holds Lock 1, waits for Lock 2
Thread B holds Lock 2, waits for Lock 1
Result: Neither can proceed → deadlock

Avoiding Deadlock:

- Acquire locks in a fixed global order

- Use try-lock with timeout and backoff

- Limit number of held locks at one time

Recognizing and addressing race conditions, deadlocks, and synchronization challenges are indispensable skills for developing reliable concurrent software. Employing proper synchronization primitives, following disciplined resource acquisition protocols, and designing data access patterns thoughtfully prevent these common pitfalls and enable programs to exploit concurrency safely and effectively.

7.4 Modern Hardware: Multicore, Caches, and SIMD

Modern central processing units (CPUs) have evolved into highly complex architectures designed to maximize computational throughput and efficiency. Key advances include the integration of multiple processor cores, hierarchical cache memory systems, and instruction sets that enable data-level parallelism known as Single Instruction Multiple Data (SIMD). Understanding these features is fundamental for optimizing software to fully leverage available hardware resources.

At the core of a modern CPU are multiple executing cores, each capable of performing independent operations. A core contains arithmetic logic units (ALUs) responsible for executing arithmetic and logical instructions, registers that provide fast local storage for immediate values, and control units that manage instruction fetching, decoding, and execution sequencing. Multiple cores within a CPU chip operate concurrently, allowing true parallel execution of multiple threads or processes. This multicore design addresses performance demands by scaling computation vertically within a single physical processor.

Beyond the cores, CPUs incorporate several levels of cache memory, which act as fast intermediate storage to reduce delays associated with accessing slower main memory (RAM). Cache memory is organized hierarchically into Level 1 (L1), Level 2 (L2), and Level 3 (L3) caches, each increasing in size and latency. L1 caches are the smallest and fastest, located closest to each core, while L3 caches are larger and shared across cores, providing a reservoir for data that is less frequently accessed but still benefits from faster retrieval than main memory.

The following table summarizes typical cache characteristics in modern multicore processors:

Cache Level	Typical Size	Latency (cycles)	Scope
L1 Cache	32–64 KB	1–4	Private to each core
L2 Cache	256 KB – 1 MB	10–20	Private to each core
L3 Cache	2–32 MB	20–50	Shared among all cores

Table 7.4: *Cache hierarchy characteristics in modern CPUs*

Each cache is divided into cache lines, which are fixed-size blocks of contiguous memory typically 64 bytes in length. Data is transferred between memory and cache at the granularity of cache lines. Efficient use of caches relies heavily on two principles: temporal and spatial locality. Temporal locality refers to the tendency of a program to access the same memory locations repeatedly within short time intervals, allowing data to remain in the cache for reuse. Spatial locality describes the tendency of programs to access memory addresses sequentially or near each other, facilitating the loading of neighboring data into cache lines in a single operation. Optimizing a program's memory access patterns to maximize these localities significantly improves cache hit rates and thus overall execution speed.

In addition to multicore and cache organization, modern processors often support SIMD instructions, which allow a single instruction to operate simultaneously on multiple data elements. Vectorization leverages SIMD by processing multiple pieces of data in parallel using wide vector registers. For example, a SIMD instruction can add multiple pairs of integers or floating-point values at once, effectively multiplying computational throughput without increasing core frequency or consuming extra power.

SIMD instruction sets vary across architectures, including Intel's SSE, AVX series, and ARM's NEON. Programmers can explicitly use SIMD intrinsics—special function calls provided by compilers—to write vectorized code, or rely on compilers' auto-vectorization capabilities.

Consider the following example using Intel intrinsics in C to perform element-wise addition of two arrays using SIMD instructions:

```c
#include <immintrin.h>

void simd_add(float* a, float* b, float* result, int n) {
    int i;
    for (i = 0; i <= n - 8; i += 8) {
```

169

```
    __m256 vec_a = _mm256_loadu_ps(&a[i]);
    __m256 vec_b = _mm256_loadu_ps(&b[i]);
    __m256 vec_res = _mm256_add_ps(vec_a, vec_b);
    _mm256_storeu_ps(&result[i], vec_res);
  }
  for (; i < n; i++) { // Handle remaining elements
    result[i] = a[i] + b[i];
  }
}
```

Here, the function processes eight floating-point elements simultaneously by utilizing 256-bit AVX registers (`__m256`). The first loop vectorizes addition in blocks of eight, while the second loop handles any leftover elements.

The performance improvements obtained through vectorization are substantial, with benchmarks frequently showing speedups of up to 4x to 8x on SIMD-capable processors compared to scalar code. Such gains arise from executing multiple operations per instruction cycle, reducing the total number of instructions and associated overhead.

Memory bandwidth and latency remain critical factors influencing overall system throughput. Although caches alleviate the penalty of accessing slower main memory, the rate at which data moves between memory and CPU still limits achievable performance, particularly for data-intensive workloads. If the program's working set size exceeds cache capacity or exhibits poor locality, frequent cache misses cause stalled CPU cycles while waiting for data retrieval. Techniques such as prefetching—where the processor anticipates future data accesses—and optimizing data alignment to cache lines help mitigate these delays.

Effective hardware-aware optimization requires a comprehensive approach that aligns software design with hardware capabilities. Key practices include structuring data for contiguous memory access to exploit spatial locality, minimizing memory access latency by reusing data to leverage temporal locality, parallelizing tasks across multiple cores to improve throughput, and employing vectorized instructions for data-parallel computations. Profiling tools can assist in identifying cache misses and vectorization hotspots, guiding targeted refinements.

Modern CPUs combine multicore parallelism, hierarchical caches, and SIMD vectorization to deliver unparalleled computational performance. Software that conscientiously considers these hardware features, optimizes memory access patterns, and leverages vectorization can achieve significant efficiency gains, fully exploiting the rich parallelism latent in contemporary processor designs.

7.5 Techniques and Tools for Scaling

Scaling software performance to handle increasing workload demands or fully utilize modern hardware involves a combination of architectural principles, efficient programming models, and supportive tools. Effective scaling harnesses parallelism at multiple levels, carefully manages system resources, and emphasizes safe concurrency to minimize errors while maximizing throughput. This section presents key approaches and frameworks for achieving scalable and efficient code execution, focusing on practical techniques that balance performance and maintainability.

A primary technique for scaling performance is the use of parallel libraries and frameworks that abstract the complexities of low-level thread management, synchronization, and workload distribution. These libraries provide structured APIs and runtime support to

express concurrency and parallelism with minimal boilerplate while
adapting to underlying hardware characteristics. Many such frameworks are designed specifically for shared-memory multicore systems
or distributed computing clusters.

Library/Framework	Primary Use Case	Key Features
OpenMP	Shared-memory parallelism for C, C++, Fortran	Compiler directives for easy parallel loops; task parallelism; well suited for straightforward loop parallelization
Intel Threading Building Blocks (TBB)	Shared-memory task-based parallelism	High-level task scheduling; scalable concurrent containers; work stealing for load balancing
Message Passing Interface (MPI)	Distributed-memory parallel computing	Explicit message passing for communication across cluster nodes; suitable for large-scale HPC applications
CUDA	GPU programming	Data-parallelism on NVIDIA GPUs; fine-grained control over threads and memory hierarchy
OpenCL	Heterogeneous parallelism across CPUs, GPUs, FPGAs	Portable parallel programming model; kernels executed concurrently across devices

Table 7.5: *Comparison of popular parallel programming libraries and frameworks*

Thread pools constitute an essential tool for scaling concurrent execution efficiently within shared-memory systems. Instead of creating and
destroying threads dynamically for every unit of work—which causes
considerable overhead—thread pools maintain a fixed or dynamically
adjustable set of worker threads. These threads await incoming tasks
dispatched to a task queue, enabling rapid reuse of threads and reducing latency in responding to work requests. Thread pools also facilitate
controlling the degree of concurrency, preventing thread proliferation

172

that can exhaust system resources or degrade performance.

Using thread pools involves submitting discrete units of work (tasks) to the pool, which are then executed asynchronously by worker threads. Thread pools often integrate queue management, load balancing, and synchronization utilities, making them suitable for complex applications requiring scalable parallelism.

The following example in C++ using the standard library demonstrates a simple thread pool pattern where tasks are asynchronously submitted and executed:

```
#include <iostream>
#include <vector>
#include <future>
#include <numeric>

int compute_sum(int start, int end) {
    int sum = 0;
    for (int i = start; i < end; ++i)
        sum += i;
    return sum;
}

int main() {
    std::vector<std::future<int>> futures;
    int chunk_size = 1000;
    int total = 0;
    for (int i = 0; i < 10000; i += chunk_size) {
        futures.push_back(std::async(std::launch::async, compute_sum, i,
        i+chunk_size));
    }
    for (auto &fut : futures) {
        total += fut.get();
    }
    std::cout << "Sum: " << total << std::endl;
    return 0;
}
```

This code splits a summation task into chunks executed concurrently

173

via asynchronous futures, managed by an internal thread pool. The
program aggregates the results to produce the final total.

Another principle critical to safe and scalable concurrent programming
is immutability. Immutable data structures are those whose state cannot be altered once created. By eliminating shared mutable state, immutability substantially reduces the risk of race conditions and synchronization errors. Programs built around immutable objects avoid
many concurrency pitfalls and enable safer parallel execution without
costly locking mechanisms.

Implementing immutable objects typically involves designing data
containers that provide no setters or mutators and produce new instances when modifications are required. The following Java example
illustrates an immutable point object:

```java
public final class Point {
    private final int x;
    private final int y;

    public Point(int x, int y) {
        this.x = x;
        this.y = y;
    }

    public Point move(int dx, int dy) {
        return new Point(x + dx, y + dy);
    }

    public int getX() { return x; }
    public int getY() { return y; }
}
```

Since the `Point` class has no mutators altering state, instances are inherently thread-safe and can be freely shared across concurrent tasks
without synchronization.

174

Adhering to guidelines for safe concurrency furthers the development of maintainable and scalable software. Major principles include minimizing shared mutable state, favoring thread-safe libraries and data structures, structuring code to reduce critical sections, and clearly defining ownership of data and resources. Additionally, leveraging high-level concurrency abstractions—such as futures, promises, and software transactional memory—simplifies reasoning about complex interactions and mitigates common errors.

Best practices for scaling concurrent software emphasize modular design, comprehensive testing under concurrency stress, profiling to identify performance bottlenecks, and judicious use of synchronization to balance safety with throughput. Documentation and consistent coding standards also play pivotal roles in managing complexity as codebases grow.

Workload distribution strategies further optimize scalable execution by efficiently partitioning computational tasks. Common approaches include data parallelism—dividing datasets into chunks processed simultaneously—and task parallelism—structuring programs as interdependent or independent tasks executed concurrently. Hybrid strategies combine both to adapt to diverse problem domains.

Employing appropriate parallel libraries, managing threads efficiently with thread pools, adopting immutability where feasible, and strategically distributing workload form the foundation for constructing high-performance, scalable, and thread-safe software. Combining these techniques with thorough testing, profiling, and feedback leads to resilient applications that fully exploit hardware capabilities while minimizing concurrency hazards.

Strategy	Description	Advantages
Data Parallelism	Splits data into discrete segments, each processed by separate tasks	Intuitive for large datasets; facilitates SIMD and vectorization
Task Parallelism	Divides computation into independent or loosely coupled tasks	Flexible for heterogeneous workloads; adapts to complex control flow
Pipeline Parallelism	Organizes tasks into sequential stages processed concurrently	Suitable for stream processing; reduces latency
Hybrid Parallelism	Combines multiple partitioning techniques	Leverages strengths of each; adapts to varied workloads

Table 7.6: *Workload distribution strategies for scalable software*

8

Profiling, Debugging, and Testing for Performance

This chapter emphasizes the importance of profiling, debugging, and testing as essential tools for optimizing software performance. It discusses how profiling tools help identify bottlenecks by providing detailed insights into code execution and resource utilization. Debugging techniques focus on root cause analysis, tracebacks, and recognizing performance-specific bug patterns. The chapter stresses the use of automated testing and benchmarks to ensure consistent performance improvements and detect regressions. It concludes with a structured workflow for iterative performance analysis, implementation, validation, and documentation.

8.1   What Is Profiling?

Profiling is a systematic technique for analyzing a program during execution to identify parts of the code that consume significant resources
or cause performance degradation. It involves collecting detailed data
on how a program operates in terms of time spent executing specific
functions, memory usage, input/output (I/O) operations, and other
performance-related metrics. By revealing "hotspots," or sections of
code responsible for the majority of resource consumption, profiling
enables developers to focus optimization efforts precisely where they
will be most effective.

The primary purpose of profiling is to provide empirical evidence
about a program's runtime behavior. While intuition or code inspection may suggest potential performance issues, profiling delivers objective measurements that quantify the time and resource demands of various code segments. It answers critical questions such
as which functions are called most often, which ones take the longest
to execute, and how different components interact with hardware resources like memory and disk. This level of insight is essential for pinpointing bottlenecks—those limiting factors that reduce overall system
efficiency—and for verifying whether optimization efforts actually improve performance.

Profiling techniques generally fall into several categories based on the
type of resource usage they measure. Table 8.1 summarizes the main
kinds of profiling commonly employed in software performance analysis:

The general process of profiling involves several distinct steps. First,
the program must be prepared or instrumented to collect profiling

Profiling Type	Measurement Focus	Common Techniques
CPU Profiling	Measures processor time spent in functions or code blocks.	Sampling profilers, instrumented code, call graph analysis
Memory Profiling	Tracks memory allocation, deallocation, leaks, and peak usage.	Heap analysis, allocation tracking, garbage collection metrics
I/O Profiling	Monitors input/output operations, such as file reads/writes and network activity.	System call tracing, event logging, throughput measuring

Table 8.1: *Summary of Profiling Types and Techniques*

data, either through automatic insertion of monitoring code, sampling of CPU registers, or using external monitoring tools. Secondly, the program is executed using typical inputs or workloads while the profiling system records relevant data on performance metrics. Finally, the collected data must be analyzed to identify bottlenecks or inefficient patterns. This process can be outlined in pseudocode as follows:

```
initialize profiler
instrument code to collect desired metrics
execute program with representative input
gather profiling data during execution
analyze profiling data to identify hotspots
generate report summarizing findings
```

Profiling delivers multiple significant benefits during software development and maintenance. It guides optimizations toward critical sections that have the greatest impact on performance, preventing unnecessary or premature tuning of less important code areas. Profiling also reduces debugging time by revealing hidden bottlenecks that may not be evident from static code analysis. As a feedback mechanism, it helps verify whether changes improve performance or introduce regressions. Overall, profiling supports efficient use of development resources by focusing efforts on high-value improvements.

Various tools exist to support profiling across programming languages

and platforms. Table 8.2 compares several commonly used profilers
that exemplify different approaches and use cases:

Tool	Profiling Type(s)	Supported Languages	Typical Use Cases
gprof	CPU, call graph	C, C++	Profiling compiled binaries for function-level hotspots
VisualVM	CPU, memory, threads	Java	Analysis of JVM applications with GUI visualization
Perf	CPU, hardware events	Linux-native binaries	Low-level hardware performance monitoring on Linux
Valgrind	Memory, profiling	C, C++	Memory leak detection and cache/memory profiling

Table 8.2: *Common Profiling Tools and Their Features*

An illustrative example of profiling output demonstrates how detailed
information can be presented to the developer. Consider the following
sample report excerpt from a CPU profiler that shows function names,
execution times, and call counts:

```
Function          Calls   Total Time (ms)   Time per Call (ms)
-----------------------------------------------------------------
process_data      5000         1200             0.24
parse_input       20000        950              0.0475
update_statistics 15000        500              0.033
render_output     3000         300              0.10
```

This output clearly identifies process_data as the function consuming
the greatest total execution time, signaling a key target for optimization.

Despite its utility, profiling has inherent limitations that must be ac-
knowledged. Profiling introduces runtime overhead because monitoring code or sampling interrupts program execution, which can slightly

alter performance characteristics. Sampling-based profilers can miss short-lived or infrequent events, leading to less accurate data if the sample size is inadequate. Furthermore, profiling results are only as relevant as the workload used during data collection; unrealistic or unrepresentative inputs can produce misleading insights. To overcome these issues, profiling should be combined with other analysis techniques and repeated under varying conditions.

Adhering to best practices enhances the quality and usefulness of profiling. Running profiling sessions with representative workloads ensures measurements reflect real-world usage. Focusing analysis on critical application modules or suspected bottlenecks avoids overwhelming volumes of data. Repeated profiling before and after changes helps track improvements and detect regressions. Additionally, maintaining awareness of profiling overhead and understanding the underlying hardware and language runtime assists in accurate interpretation of results.

Profiling is an indispensable practice in the performance optimization workflow, offering detailed, quantitative feedback on where time and resources are spent during execution. By methodically applying profiling tools and techniques, developers can systematically uncover bottlenecks and prioritize targeted improvements, ultimately producing software that meets performance requirements with efficiency and precision.

8.2 Performance Profiling Tools Overview

Performance profiling tools are essential software utilities that help developers investigate the runtime behavior of their programs and identify where optimization efforts should be concentrated. For beginners, selecting accessible and well-documented profiling tools is critical to understanding performance insights without being overwhelmed by complexity. This section provides an overview of some popular, beginner-friendly profilers and monitors frequently used in industry and academia to measure performance characteristics in diverse programming environments.

Profiling tools generally differ in the scope of metrics they collect, their ease of use, and the programming languages and platforms they support. Some tools focus on CPU usage and function execution time, while others provide detailed memory usage, threading information, or hardware-level event tracing. Modern tools often provide graphical user interfaces (GUIs) to visualize profiling data, making it easier for newcomers to interpret results effectively.

One widely used CPU profiling tool is gprof, which serves as a practical starting point for profiling compiled C or C++ applications. Table 8.3 summarizes the primary features of gprof:

Feature	Description
Supported Languages	C, C++ (compiled with GCC)
Profiling Type	CPU time, call graph analysis
Instrumentation Method	Program compiled with -pg flag
Output Format	Text reports showing execution times and call counts
Typical Use Cases	Identifying hot functions and understanding call relationships
Beginner Friendliness	Moderate; requires recompilation and command-line usage

Table 8.3: *Overview of gprof Profiling Tool*

gprof operates by compiling the target program with special flags that automatically insert instrumentation code. When the program runs, it records function entry and exit times along with how functions call each other. At program termination, gprof generates reports quantifying total time spent per function and call graph statistics, facilitating identification of the primary computationally intensive areas.

For Java developers, `VisualVM` is a popular GUI-based profiling and monitoring tool providing an accessible interface to observe CPU usage, memory consumption, and thread activity in Java Virtual Machine (JVM) processes. Table 8.4 highlights how `VisualVM` compares to other Java profilers:

Tool	CPU Profiling	Memory Profiling	Additional Features
VisualVM	Yes (sampling and instrumentation)	Yes (heap analysis, allocation tracking)	Thread monitoring, plugin support, snapshot comparison
JProfiler	Yes	Yes	Advanced UI, integration with IDEs, rich analysis tools
YourKit Java Profiler	Yes	Yes	Minimal overhead, detailed allocation graphs, smart telemetry

Table 8.4: *Comparison of VisualVM with Other Java Profiling Tools*

`VisualVM` runs alongside JVM applications and collects real-time data with minimal configuration. Its graphical interface presents CPU and memory profiling information as charts and tables, supporting beginners in quickly identifying performance hotspots and memory leaks.

On Linux systems, the `perf` tool stands out as a powerful command-line utility that leverages hardware performance counters to provide low-level profiling data. Table 8.5 summarizes its characteristics:

While `perf` requires understanding of hardware-level events and familiarity with Linux commands, it provides detailed insights that surpass many other profilers in resolution and accuracy.

Feature	Description
Supported Platform	Linux (kernel 2.6.31 and later)
Profiling Type	CPU cycles, cache misses, branch mispredictions, context switches
Instrumentation Method	Hardware performance counters, event sampling
Output Format	Text/graphical reports, flame graphs with external parsers
Typical Use Cases	Low-level system profiling, detecting CPU and memory bottlenecks
Beginner Friendliness	Advanced; command-line interface with extensive options

Table 8.5: *Overview of Linux perf Profiling Tool*

Instrumenting code for profiling often requires small modifications or compiling with special flags. The following examples illustrate how to prepare a simple C program for profiling with gprof and how to enable Java profiling with VisualVM:

```
gcc -pg -o myprogram myprogram.c
./myprogram
gprof myprogram gmon.out > analysis.txt
```

The above commands enable profiling instrumentation via the -pg compiler flag, run the program to generate runtime data into gmon.out, and then create a human-readable analysis report.

For Java applications, one typically starts the JVM with the -agentlib:jvisualvm flag or runs the application normally and connects VisualVM to it via its interface, requiring no code modifications.

Profiling tools capture several crucial metrics that help developers understand performance behavior. Key metrics include:

- **CPU Time:** The total time a processor spends executing code within a function or module.

- **Function Call Counts:** How often each function is invoked during program execution.

184

- **Memory Usage:** Amount of heap and stack memory allocated, used, and freed by the program.

- **I/O Activity:** Counts and durations of file, network, or database input/output operations.

- **Thread and Process States:** Information on concurrency, synchronization delays, and context switches.

Interpreting profiling data involves identifying "hot" functions or code regions that consume significant CPU time or memory. Functions with high CPU usage but infrequent calls may indicate complex computations, while those called extensively but consuming less time might suggest inefficiencies in repeated operations. Memory profiling can uncover leaks, excessive allocations, or fragmentation. Evaluating I/O metrics helps detect bottlenecks caused by slow disk access or network latency.

To illustrate, below is a representative excerpt from a profiling report similar to one generated by gprof or VisualVM:

Function	Calls	Total Time (ms)	Avg Time per Call (ms)
compute_results	15000	1250	0.083
read_input	30000	600	0.020
update_cache	10000	450	0.045
save_output	5000	300	0.060

Functions compute_results and read_input clearly dominate runtime, indicating priority areas for optimization.

Although profiling tools provide indispensable insights, their outputs carry limitations that users must consider. Profiling incurs overhead, as monitoring interrupts normal program execution or instruments extra code, which can influence timing and behavior. Sampling profilers may miss rare or short-lived events, reducing data completeness. Fur-

185

thermore, profiling results heavily depend on workload representativeness; profiling with unrealistic or incomplete input data can lead to misleading conclusions. Consequently, profiling should be conducted under varied and realistic test conditions, complementing other analysis approaches like code inspection and benchmarking.

Selecting the most suitable profiling tool depends on several factors including programming language, execution environment, performance goals, and user expertise. Languages like C and C++ typically utilize tools such as gprof, Valgrind, or perf, while Java developers benefit from JVM-centric tools like VisualVM or commercial profilers. For applications requiring low-level hardware event analysis, perf or similar system profilers are appropriate. When ease of use and graphical feedback are priorities, GUI-based profilers such as VisualVM or alternatives tailored for specific languages provide a gentler learning curve for beginners. Ultimately, familiarity with several profiling tools equips programmers to address diverse performance challenges effectively.

8.3 Performance Debugging Techniques

Performance debugging is a critical process in software development focused on identifying, analyzing, and resolving issues that degrade the speed, responsiveness, or resource efficiency of a program. Unlike functional debugging, which addresses correctness and error states, performance debugging targets bottlenecks and inefficiencies that cause slow execution or excessive resource consumption. Applying systematic methods to detect and address performance-related bugs enables developers to optimize software behavior and improve user experience or system throughput.

A core component of performance debugging is root cause analysis, a disciplined approach to uncover the fundamental reasons underlying observed performance problems. Rather than addressing superficial symptoms such as slow response times or high CPU usage, root cause analysis seeks to isolate the specific code paths, algorithmic inefficiencies, synchronization conflicts, or memory management issues responsible. This approach typically involves collecting relevant runtime data, formulating hypotheses, and empirically validating them through targeted testing and instrumentation. Root cause analysis ensures optimized solutions that directly target the bottlenecks, avoiding wasted effort on non-critical components.

Tracebacks and profiling data provide essential evidence during performance debugging. Tracebacks, or stack traces, capture the sequence of function calls active at specific checkpoints or during exceptional events, helping to reveal where execution is concentrated. Profiling data complements tracebacks by quantifying resource usage such as CPU time, memory allocations, or I/O activity on a per-function basis. Combining stack trace information with profiling outputs allows developers to pinpoint not just where time is spent but also the call context and dependencies. A typical code snippet demonstrating the extraction of runtime stack traces and profiling data might look as follows (in Python for illustration):

```
import cProfile
import traceback

def problematic_function():
    # code suspected of causing performance issue
    pass

def main():
    profiler = cProfile.Profile()
    profiler.enable()
    try:
```

```
    problematic_function()
except Exception:
    print("Exception Traceback:")
    traceback.print_exc()
finally:
    profiler.disable()
    profiler.print_stats(sort='cumtime')

if __name__ == "__main__":
    main()
```

This example captures profiling data for the target function and prints
any raised exceptions with their stack traces, aiding in correlating runtime errors with performance behavior.

Performance bugs often manifest through identifiable patterns that recur across projects and systems. Table 8.6 organizes common performance bug patterns and their typical characteristics:

Bug Pattern	Description	Impact on Performance
Excessive Locking	Overuse or coarse-grained locking in multithreaded code	Causes contention, thread blocking, and reduced parallelism
Repeated Computations	Unnecessary recalculation of values instead of caching	Wastes CPU cycles and increases latency
Memory Leaks	Failure to release unused memory allocations	Leads to increased memory usage, paging, and eventual crashes
Inefficient Data Structures	Use of suboptimal structures for data access/modification	Increases algorithmic complexity, slows execution
Blocking I/O	Synchronous I/O operations on critical paths	Introduces delays, stalls program responsiveness
Excessive Logging	Verbose or unfiltered logging in production code	Consumes CPU and disk I/O resources unnecessarily

Table 8.6: *Common Performance Bug Patterns*

Once a performance issue is suspected, diagnostic techniques enable
developers to systematically investigate and confirm root causes. Logging critical events and timestamps provides chronological context;

188

event tracing tracks program execution flow; manual instrumentation inserts timers or counters within code to measure execution duration. These methods complement profiling tools by providing detailed insight into specific portions of code, especially when profiling tools cannot capture application-specific logic or external interactions.

Profilers are also essential debugging aids beyond initial hotspot identification. By monitoring unexpected resource usage—such as unusual spikes in memory allocation or lock contention—profilers help isolate performance bugs that may not be obvious from code inspection. Repeated profiling during iterative debugging cycles supports verification of fixes and detection of secondary issues.

A structured debugging workflow can improve efficiency and accuracy. The typical steps include:

```
detect performance degradation
collect initial profiling and tracing data
identify candidate bottlenecks or suspicious code
hypothesize root cause(s)
apply targeted instrumentation or logging
test hypothesis with controlled experiments
implement fixes or optimizations
reprofile to verify improvement
document findings and changes
```

The iterative nature of this workflow enables continuous refinement and prevents premature conclusions about problem sources.

An illustrative case study demonstrates this workflow in action. Suppose a server application experiences slow response times under load. Initial profiling reveals a function `parse_request` consuming 60% of CPU time, but the root cause is unclear. Detailed logging uncovers that the function repeatedly parses identical data due to missing caching. By introducing a cache and rerunning the profile, CPU time drops measurably, confirming the fix's effectiveness:

Function	CPU Time (ms)	Calls
Before optimization		
parse_request	12000	10000
After optimization		
parse_request	4000	10000
cache_lookup	1000	8000

This example highlights how root cause analysis combined with targeted instrumentation enables precise identification and resolution of performance bugs.

Best practices for performance debugging emphasize minimizing disruption and ensuring reliable validation. It is advisable to isolate debugging activities in development or staging environments to avoid impacting production users. Accurate measurement requires controlled test inputs and repeatable conditions. After applying fixes, rigorous remeasurement confirms that performance has improved without introducing regressions. Maintaining detailed documentation of debugging sessions preserves institutional knowledge and supports future troubleshooting.

By employing these systematic techniques—root cause analysis, stack trace and profiling data interpretation, recognition of common bug patterns, disciplined diagnostic methods, and iterative workflow adherence—developers can effectively identify and resolve performance bottlenecks. This structured approach transforms the complex task of performance debugging into a manageable and repeatable engineering practice, leading to more efficient, responsive, and robust software systems.

8.4 Automated Testing and Benchmarking

Automated testing and benchmarking are fundamental strategies for evaluating and maintaining software performance consistently and efficiently. Automating the execution of tests and benchmarks reduces human error, ensures repeatability, and facilitates frequent performance validation throughout the development lifecycle. By systematically integrating automated performance evaluations, developers gain reliable insights into how code changes impact execution speed, memory consumption, and other critical metrics, enabling prompt detection and resolution of regressions or inefficiencies.

Designing benchmarks that produce reproducible results is crucial to obtaining meaningful performance data. Reproducibility means that repeated executions under comparable conditions yield similar measurements, allowing valid comparisons over time or across software versions. To achieve this, benchmarks should be constructed with stable input data, fixed random seeds where applicable, and controlled environmental factors such as processor load, memory availability, and network conditions. Automating setup and teardown procedures further reduces variability caused by manual intervention, creating a consistent testing environment.

Managing test cases effectively plays an essential role in streamlining automated performance testing. Various test frameworks provide built-in support for organizing, executing, and reporting benchmarks. Table 8.7 lists some popular testing frameworks that facilitate automation of performance tests across programming languages:

Automating the benchmarking process involves scripting benchmark setup, execution, and result collection to minimize manual steps and

191

Framework	Language	Performance Features	Typical Use Cases
JUnit	Java	Benchmarking annotations, integration with CI	Unit and performance testing for JVM projects
pytest-benchmark	Python	Benchmark decorators, result comparison	Microbenchmarking and continuous performance tracking
Google Benchmark	C++	Precise timing, statistics support	High-resolution C++ benchmarks for algorithms
Benchmark.js	JavaScript	Load testing, asynchronous benchmarks	Web application performance measurement

Table 8.7: *Comparison of Popular Test Frameworks Supporting Automated Performance Tests*

ensure uniformity. The following illustrative Python script exemplifies automated benchmarking using the `timeit` module for measuring function execution time, capturing results, and writing them to a file:

```python
import timeit

def process_data():
    # Simulated workload: replace with actual code
    total = 0
    for i in range(10000):
        total += i * i
    return total

def run_benchmark():
    # Measure execution time over multiple runs
    times = timeit.repeat("process_data()", globals=globals(), repeat=5,
     number=10)
    avg_time = sum(times) / len(times)
    with open("benchmark_results.txt", "w") as f:
        f.write(f"Average execution time: {avg_time:.6f} seconds\n")
        f.write(f"Individual runs: {times}\n")

if __name__ == "__main__":
    run_benchmark()
```

This script runs the target function multiple times, calculates average execution time, and logs detailed run data for analysis or historical tracking.

Collecting relevant performance metrics requires appropriate instrumentation and observation tools. Execution time is typically measured using high-resolution timers provided by the runtime or operating system. Memory usage can be tracked via external profilers or runtime APIs that report heap allocation and live object counts. Monitoring CPU utilization and system-level parameters often involves interfacing with operating system performance counters or third-party libraries. Combining these metrics provides a detailed view of an application's resource consumption under benchmarked scenarios.

Ensuring benchmark result reproducibility demands controlling sources of variability. For example, random number generation should employ fixed seeds to guarantee consistent input across runs. Environmental factors such as CPU frequency scaling, background processes, and system load should be minimized or standardized. Containerization or virtualization technologies can isolate test environments, reducing external interference. Additionally, resetting caches, databases, or network connections between runs prevents stateful effects from influencing measurements. Documenting the benchmark configuration, software version, and hardware specifications further aids reproducibility and future comparisons.

Tracking performance over time enhances the ability to spot regressions and improvements. Visualization of benchmark results across software versions or configuration changes clarifies trends and anomalies. Tools and dashboards can aggregate historical test data, displaying metrics such as average execution time, throughput, and memory usage in tables, line graphs, or histograms. For example, the follow-

ing output represents a simplified tabular view of benchmark results
across four software builds:

Build Version	Avg Exec Time (s)	Memory Usage (MB)
v1.0.0	0.450	120
v1.1.0	0.430	118
v1.2.0	0.460	122
v1.3.0	0.400	115

By analyzing such data, teams can identify performance regressions—
unintentional slowdowns or increased resource consumption—and
quickly initiate remediation efforts.

Automatically detecting regressions is a key benefit of integrating automated benchmarking into development workflows. Regression tests
configured to run benchmarks on every code change or nightly build
can flag significant decreases in performance metrics. Notification systems alert developers of these events, enabling prompt investigation
before regressions affect end users. Automated regression testing complements functional testing by ensuring new features or bug fixes do
not degrade performance.

Adopting best practices for automated benchmarking facilitates scalable and reliable performance evaluation. These include defining
clear performance goals and thresholds to interpret benchmark results meaningfully, maintaining comprehensive test suites covering
representative usage patterns, and documenting test procedures and
environment configurations. Automating the entire test pipeline—
from code checkout to reporting—using continuous integration (CI)
systems guarantees consistency and expedites feedback. Periodically
auditing and updating benchmarks ensures relevance as functionality evolves. Finally, maintaining version control for test scripts and
benchmark data preserves historical context and supports collaboration among developers.

Automated testing and benchmarking therefore provide a disciplined, repeatable framework for monitoring and improving software performance. By combining careful benchmark design, robust metric collection, and continuous regression detection, developers can systematically validate optimizations, maintain high-performance standards, and minimize the risk of unnoticed degradations throughout the software lifecycle.

8.5   Workflow for Iterative Improvement

Performance optimization is best approached as an ongoing, cyclical process rather than a one-time effort. By adopting an iterative workflow, developers can systematically measure current performance, identify critical bottlenecks, apply targeted improvements, validate outcomes, and document results to inform future work. This continuous cycle facilitates progressive enhancement, prevents regressions, and ensures that optimizations remain aligned with evolving requirements and usage patterns.

The cycle begins with establishing a baseline measurement—an initial quantification of the program's performance prior to any changes. This baseline serves as a reference point to assess the effectiveness of subsequent optimizations and to detect any regressions that may arise during development. For example, a Python script using the `timeit` module can measure baseline execution time of a function:

```
import timeit

def target_function():
    # Placeholder for the function to be optimized
    total = 0
    for i in range(100000):
```

```
        total += i*i
    return total

if __name__ == "__main__":
    baseline_time = timeit.timeit("target_function()", globals=globals(),
        number=10)
    print(f"Baseline execution time over 10 runs: {baseline_time:.4f}
        seconds")
```

This code snippet captures an aggregated execution time across multiple invocations, providing a quantifiable starting point.

Following baseline measurement, the next step is to identify bottlenecks that limit performance. This involves analyzing profiling data to locate functions, loops, or operations consuming disproportionate computational resources or causing delays. Techniques include employing sampling or instrumentation profilers to gather CPU usage, memory allocation, and I/O statistics; interpreting call graphs to understand execution paths; and reviewing benchmark outputs to observe latency and throughput trends. Prioritizing optimization efforts towards the most critical bottlenecks ensures efficient use of development time and maximizes impact.

The implementation phase encompasses refactoring code and applying performance enhancements based on bottleneck analysis. Optimizations may include algorithmic improvements to reduce complexity, restructuring data handling to improve cache locality, minimizing synchronization in multithreaded contexts, or eliminating redundant computations. It is important to maintain code clarity and correctness during this phase, avoiding premature or overly aggressive optimizations that can introduce bugs or reduce maintainability.

Once changes are applied, re-measuring performance through rerunning benchmarks verifies whether optimizations deliver anticipated

196

improvements without compromising correctness. For consistency, the same benchmarking approach used during baseline measurement should be repeated, ideally automated for repeatability. The following example reruns the previous benchmark to capture post-optimization execution time:

```
if __name__ == "__main__":
    optimized_time = timeit.timeit("target_function()", globals=globals()
    , number=10)
    print(f"Post-optimization execution time: {optimized_time:.4f}
    seconds")
    improvement = ((baseline_time - optimized_time) / baseline_time) *
    100
    print(f"Performance improvement: {improvement:.2f}%")
```

Calculating improvement as a percentage quantifies the optimization's effectiveness, providing objective feedback.

Documentation is an essential final step in this workflow. Recording the nature of changes implemented, profiling metrics before and after optimization, encountered challenges, and lessons learned creates valuable reference material for future development. Clear documentation supports knowledge transfer among team members, facilitates regression diagnosis, and informs decision-making about further enhancements or trade-offs. Documentation formats can include code comments, commit messages, performance reports, or dedicated design documents.

The iterative nature of performance improvement can be represented as a flowchart with the following steps:

```
START
   ↓
Measure baseline performance
   ↓
Analyze profiling and benchmark data
```

```
     ↓
Identify bottlenecks
     ↓
Implement optimizations
     ↓
Re-measure and validate changes
     ↓
Document results
     ↓
Repeat cycle or END
```

This cycle repeats regularly during development until performance goals are met or resources are exhausted.

Automating this workflow enhances efficiency and reliability. Integrating benchmarking scripts, profiling tools, result aggregation, and reporting into automated pipelines reduces manual effort, minimizes human error, and provides timely feedback. Automation tools can schedule tests, run performance suites on varying hardware or configurations, generate comparison reports, and trigger alerts if regressions occur. Comprehensive automation also enables scaling performance testing to larger codebases and concurrent projects.

Integrating performance testing into continuous integration (CI) pipelines further strengthens quality assurance. By running automated benchmarks alongside functional tests during code integration, teams receive immediate insights into the impact of code changes on performance. This proactive detection of regressions or unexpected slowdowns prevents degradation from accumulating unnoticed. CI systems facilitate systematic version control of tests, environment standardization, and seamless collaboration between developers and operations teams. The continuous feedback loop established by CI promotes a culture of ongoing performance awareness and incremental improvement.

In sum, iterative performance improvement is a structured methodology for systematically enhancing software efficiency. Through cycles of careful measurement, focused optimization, rigorous validation, and meticulous documentation, developers systematically evolve applications to meet performance objectives while maintaining stability and maintainability. Automation and integration with development workflows amplify these benefits, enabling sustainable, scalable, and reproducible performance engineering.

9

Special Considerations in Performance Optimization

This chapter explores unique challenges and opportunities when optimizing performance on mobile and embedded devices, considering constraints like energy consumption and limited resources. It discusses the importance of energy-efficient coding practices to extend battery life and reduce power usage. The chapter examines how to balance performance enhancements with security, highlighting potential trade-offs and best practices. It covers build and compiler optimizations, including flags and techniques for creating optimized release versions. Finally, it presents real-world case studies demonstrating successful optimization strategies tailored to specific hardware and application needs.

9.1 Performance on Mobile and Embedded Devices

Mobile and embedded devices encompass a broad spectrum of computing platforms characterized by significant heterogeneity in their hardware capabilities and operational constraints. This diversity arises from the wide range of application contexts, usage scenarios, form factors, and power sources. Mobile devices typically include smartphones, tablets, and wearable technology, whereas embedded systems range from simple microcontrollers in appliances to complex processors in automotive and industrial equipment. Understanding the distinct performance characteristics and limitations of these devices is essential for effective optimization.

The heterogeneity of mobile and embedded devices is expressed in various dimensions, including processor architecture, memory availability, battery capacity, input/output interfaces, and specialized hardware components. For instance, some devices employ ARM-based low-power CPUs optimized for energy efficiency, while others utilize more powerful processors with additional cores or higher clock speeds. Similarly, memory configurations may range from kilobytes of static RAM in microcontrollers to several gigabytes of RAM in smartphones. Device-specific features such as sensors, connectivity options, and accelerators contribute further variability. Consequently, software designed for this domain must be adaptable to a wide spectrum of hardware profiles and resource constraints.

Central to the design of mobile and embedded systems are inherent hardware limitations that significantly impact performance optimization opportunities. Reduced CPU performance relative to desktop or

202

server-class processors is common, as these devices prioritize energy efficiency and thermal management over raw computational throughput. Memory capacity is often limited, with embedded devices sometimes constrained to just a few megabytes or less of storage and volatile memory. Battery capacity combined with power consumption requirements imposes strict energy budgets, which mandate judicious use of computational and communication resources. Smaller screen sizes and varying input modalities such as touch, buttons, or voice interfaces further influence software design and resource allocation.

These constraints necessitate careful consideration when developing software, as inefficient use of CPU cycles, memory, or input/output operations can rapidly degrade user experience through sluggish response times, excessive battery drain, or unresponsiveness. Performance optimization thus transcends traditional goals of speed and must include metrics such as energy efficiency and responsiveness tailored to resource restrictions. Additionally, mobile and embedded devices frequently operate under real-time requirements and environmental constraints, further complicating optimization strategies.

Despite these limitations, mobile and embedded platforms present unique avenues for performance enhancement through device-specific hardware features. Many devices incorporate hardware accelerators such as Graphics Processing Units (GPUs), Digital Signal Processors (DSPs), and video encoders/decoders designed to execute specialized tasks more efficiently than general-purpose CPUs. Offloading computationally intensive functions such as image processing, audio decoding, or machine learning inference to these components enables substantial performance gains and power savings.

For example, leveraging a GPU for parallelizable tasks can dramatically reduce execution time relative to serial CPU computation while also consuming less energy per operation. Similarly, DSPs excel at handling signal transformations and filtering tasks with minimal power usage. Hardware video encoders enable rapid media compression without taxing the main processor. Exploiting these accelerators requires understanding their programming interfaces and performance characteristics, as well as judicious partitioning of computations to balance workload and minimize overhead.

To optimize for limited resources, several programming techniques and architectural considerations have proven effective in mobile and embedded contexts. Data compression algorithms reduce memory footprint and communication overhead by encoding data in compact forms, thereby decreasing bandwidth requirements and storage consumption. Using lightweight data structures that minimize memory usage and access costs can prevent unnecessary memory allocation and cache misses.

Power-aware programming practices are pivotal. These include minimizing the frequency and duration of CPU activity through batching operations to process multiple data items collectively, thus reducing the overhead of waking the processor from low-power states repeatedly. Scheduling background tasks to run only when the device is charging or connected to a network prevents unnecessary battery depletion. Avoiding busy-wait loops and employing sleep mechanisms can further conserve power. Selecting algorithms that prioritize early termination when the desired result is found or approximate solutions are acceptable reduces computational effort.

Consider the following programming example demonstrating batching operations and minimizing background activity to conserve power:

Table 9.1: *Device Classes: Hardware Specifications, Power Budgets, and Optimization Considerations*

Device Class	CPU	Memory	Power Budget	Optimization Focus
Smartphones	Multi-core ARM CPUs (1–3 GHz)	2–12 GB RAM	2000–4000 mAh battery	Performance and energy balance, GPU acceleration, network efficiency
Wearables	Low-power ARM Cortex-M	256 KB–1 MB RAM	200–500 mAh battery	Ultra-low power consumption, minimal latency, compressed data handling
IoT Sensors	Microcontrollers (8–32 bit)	<256 KB	Often energy-harvested or small batteries	Minimal CPU cycles, aggressive sleep states, lightweight communication
Embedded Systems	Variety of processors including ARM, MIPS	128 MB–GB range	Often wired power or large batteries	Responsiveness, deterministic behavior, hardware acceleration
Tablets	Similar to smartphones but generally higher specs	3–16 GB RAM	4000–8000 mAh battery	Graphics and UI performance, multitasking efficiency

```cpp
void processSensorDataBatch(std::vector<SensorData>& dataBatch) {
    // Process all data at once to minimize wake-up overhead
    for (const auto& data : dataBatch) {
        analyze(data);
    }
    // Enter low-power mode after processing
    enterLowPowerMode();
}

void backgroundTaskScheduler() {
    if (isNetworkAvailable() && isDeviceCharging()) {
        performBackgroundSync();
    }
    else {
        deferBackgroundTasks();
    }
}
```

This example shows deferring non-essential tasks until favorable conditions occur (e.g., charging state), which helps reduce unnecessary power consumption. Batching sensor data reduces the frequency of activating the CPU, allowing it to remain in energy-saving states longer.

Hardware acceleration opportunities abound in modern mobile and embedded platforms. Graphics Processing Units (GPUs) provide massively parallel architectures tailored to rendering and image processing but are increasingly leveraged for general-purpose computation such as physics simulations and neural network inference. Digital Signal Processors specialize in real-time processing of audio, video, and sensor signals with low latency and energy use. Hardware encoders and decoders expedite video compression and decompression, critical for streaming and media applications prevalent on mobile devices.

Exploiting these accelerators requires programming models supporting parallelism and hardware-specific APIs such as OpenCL, Vulkan, or proprietary SDKs. Efficient use of these resources can yield orders of magnitude improvement in throughput and energy efficiency compared to equivalent computations executed on the main CPU.

User interface design in mobile and embedded contexts must adapt to constrained display sizes, varying screen resolutions, and diverse input methods including touch, stylus, keyboard, or voice commands. Optimizing UI performance involves minimizing unnecessary redraws, caching graphical assets, and efficiently managing input event processing. Responsive design principles ensure usability and smooth interactions regardless of screen dimension or orientation, thereby enhancing perceived performance.

Maintaining performance across a heterogeneous device landscape necessitates thoughtful trade-offs between power consumption and resource utilization. The following table contrasts typical scenarios where performance improvements correspond to increased power consumption, alongside strategies to balance these concerns.

Ensuring consistent performance across this wide array of device profiles requires rigorous testing on multiple hardware platforms. Best practices include maintaining a representative set of devices covering various CPU types, memory sizes, operating system versions, and display configurations. Automated testing frameworks and performance profiling tools assist in identifying bottlenecks and regressions specific to particular devices.

Developers should also prioritize modular and configurable code that can adapt to runtime hardware detection, enabling activation or deactivation of features based on resource availability. Emulators and simulators provide preliminary testing environments but may not fully replicate power consumption characteristics or real-world constraints and should be complemented with physical device testing. Ensuring

Table 9.2: *Trade-offs between Performance and Power Consumption*

Scenario	Effect on Performance	Power Consumption and Mitigation Strategies
Increasing CPU clock speed	Faster execution times	Higher dynamic power; balanced by using dynamic frequency scaling and throttling
Using multiple cores in parallel	Reduced latency and higher throughput	Increased total power; use thread affinity and prioritize critical tasks
High-frequency sensor polling	Real-time responsiveness	Continuous CPU wake-ups drain power; implement event-driven triggers and batching
Continuous GPS usage for location tracking	Accurate location updates	High power drain; apply adaptive sampling and geofencing to limit use
Rendering complex graphics at high frame rate	Smooth animations and UI	GPU power spikes; employ frame rate caps and level-of-detail rendering

smooth user experiences across heterogeneous devices is a fundamental aspect of mobile and embedded system optimization.

9.2 Energy Efficiency and Optimization

In modern mobile and embedded devices, energy efficiency is a paramount concern that directly impacts device usability, operational costs, and environmental sustainability. Power conservation extends battery life, enabling longer periods between charges and improving user experience, particularly in portable systems where access to power sources may be limited. Embedded systems often run unattended for extended durations on constrained power budgets, requiring judicious consumption of energy. Programmers therefore play a critical role in minimizing the energy footprint of software by writing efficient code and designing systems that consciously account for power usage.

Efficient code execution reduces the cumulative energy expended during computation and data movement. Optimized algorithms streamline operations, decreasing the total number of CPU cycles required, which lowers dynamic power consumption. Reducing memory usage and avoiding inefficient data accesses diminishes memory subsystem activity, which also contributes to energy savings. Minimizing unnecessary sensor activations, background processes, and network transmissions further conserves device power. Collectively, these practices extend battery life, decrease heat generation, and improve system reliability.

Techniques for power conservation encompass a range of hardware and software strategies. The table below delineates commonly employed methods:

Designing power-aware algorithms involves structuring computations to minimize energy usage without sacrificing necessary performance or correctness. Early exit conditions allow an algorithm to terminate as soon as a desired result or threshold is achieved, avoiding superfluous processing. Batching inputs and outputs reduces the frequency of activating processing units and communication interfaces, enabling extended time in low-power states. Workload reduction through approximation, resolution scaling, or selective computation optimizes for energy without significantly degrading output quality.

Consider the following code example illustrating a loop optimized for energy efficiency by combining batching and early loop exit strategies.

```
void processData(const std::vector<int>& inputData) {
    const int batchSize = 50;
```

209

Table 9.3: *Power Conservation Techniques in Mobile and Embedded Systems*

Technique	Description
CPU Throttling	Dynamically reducing processor frequency and voltage to lower power draw during idle or low-utilization periods
Background Task Management	Scheduling non-critical jobs during charging or connectivity periods to avoid frequent wake-ups
Sensor Access Minimization	Reducing sampling rates or turning off sensors when not needed to save power
Batching Operations	Aggregating data or computations to execute in bursts rather than continuously
Low-power Sleep Modes	Leveraging hardware-supported sleep states to reduce power when idle
Network Efficiency	Combining transmissions and employing compression to minimize radio usage
Adaptive Brightness	Adjusting screen brightness based on ambient light to reduce display power consumption
Hardware Acceleration	Using specialized hardware blocks to perform tasks more efficiently than the CPU

```
for (size_t i = 0; i < inputData.size(); i += batchSize) {
    // Process a batch of data at once
    int batchEnd = std::min(i + batchSize, inputData.size());
    bool exitEarly = false;
    for (size_t j = i; j < batchEnd; ++j) {
        if (inputData[j] < 0) {
            // Early exit condition met; stop processing further
            exitEarly = true;
            break;
        }
        performComputation(inputData[j]);
    }
    if (exitEarly) {
        break;
    }
    // Optionally, enter low-power mode between batches
    enterLowPowerState();
}
}
```

Here, data is processed in fixed-size batches to minimize the overhead from frequent CPU wake-ups. The inner loop can exit early if a negative value is encountered, preventing unnecessary iterations. Between batches, invoking a low-power state routine helps conserve energy by reducing CPU activity.

Beyond software techniques, leveraging hardware features is essential for optimizing energy efficiency. Modern processors support various low-power modes and adaptive performance capabilities that dynamically adjust operational parameters such as clock rates and voltages based on workload. Utilizing hardware acceleration for specific tasks like cryptography, media encoding, or machine learning inference delegates work to more energy-efficient specialized units. Effective exploitation of these features necessitates profiling and tuning software to align operations with hardware capabilities and constraints.

Measurement and monitoring of energy usage are critical for informed optimization. Several tools are available to assist developers in quantifying power consumption and identifying hotspots:

These tools enable developers to collect empirical data about energy consumption associated with different code paths, system configurations, and usage patterns, informing targeted optimizations.

Balancing performance improvements with power consumption remains a nuanced challenge. Performance optimizations such as increasing CPU frequency, spawning multiple threads, or employing high-resolution polling can elevate power usage significantly. The following table presents specific scenarios illustrating these trade-offs and strategies to mitigate excessive energy consumption:

The creation of energy-efficient software must incorporate these balancing considerations to ensure user expectations for responsiveness

Table 9.4: *Energy Measurement Tools for Mobile and Embedded Devices*

Tool	Description	Supported Platforms
Trepn Profiler	Real-time profiling tool providing CPU, GPU, network, and battery metrics	Android devices
PowerTutor	Visualizes power consumption of components with app-level granularity	Android devices
Intel Power Gadget	Monitors CPU-level power and frequency statistics	Intel-based platforms
Watts Up Pro	External hardware meter capturing power usage with high accuracy	External measurement
Perf	Linux profiling framework extended for energy and power events	Linux-based systems

Table 9.5: *Performance versus Power Consumption Trade-offs*

Optimization	Performance Benefit	Power Implication and Balancing Technique
Increasing CPU frequency	Faster task completion	Higher dynamic power; use dynamic voltage and frequency scaling (DVFS) to reduce frequency when idle
Parallel multithreading	Reduced latency	Increased core utilization raises power; balance with thread scheduling policies to prevent resource contention
Continuous sensor polling	Real-time responsiveness	High energy drain; mitigate with event-triggered sampling or adaptive polling rates
Aggressive caching	Lower memory latency	Increased leakage power; balance cache size and replacement to reduce unnecessary activity
High screen brightness	Improved visibility	Greater display power draw; use adaptive brightness and dark UI themes

and functionality are met without incurring undue battery drain.

Best practices for coding and system design aimed at energy conservation include minimizing wake-up events from sleep states by batching and coalescing operations, employing efficient data structures and algorithms that reduce computational overhead, and prioritizing asynchronous and event-driven programming models to avoid busy-wait loops. User interface design should leverage layout techniques minimizing screen redraws and efficiently handling input events to limit CPU and GPU workload. Resource management must consistently release unused objects and avoid memory leaks, which lead to increased garbage collection overhead and power consumption.

The careful integration of power-awareness throughout software development—from algorithm selection and code implementation to system-level hardware utilization and user interface design—constitutes a comprehensive approach to extending battery life and reducing power consumption on modern mobile and embedded devices. This holistic focus enhances device longevity and user satisfaction while contributing to sustainability goals in computational technology.

9.3 Security and Performance Trade-offs

Optimizing software often involves balancing competing objectives, among which security and performance stand as crucial and sometimes conflicting goals. While performance enhancements aim to reduce execution time, latency, and resource consumption, security measures seek to protect data integrity, confidentiality, and system availability. This creates a delicate interplay: certain optimizations may expose vulnerabilities, whereas strong security mechanisms can degrade performance. Navigating these trade-offs requires understanding their underlying mechanisms and implications.

Performance optimization techniques such as caching and parallelism can inadvertently introduce security risks if not carefully managed. Caching data in memory or on disk improves retrieval speed but may result in sensitive information being retained longer than necessary, increasing exposure risk to unauthorized access or side-channel attacks. Similarly, parallel execution can increase complexity in synchronization, which, if flawed, may open windows for race conditions or timing attacks. Shared resources in concurrent environments may also facilitate data leakage or privilege escalation if access controls are insufficient.

Conversely, security measures inherently impose overhead. Cryptographic operations such as encryption and decryption require additional CPU cycles and memory bandwidth, often significantly slowing data processing and transmission. Authentication protocols necessitate multiple message exchanges, increasing network latency. Data validation and integrity checks consume computing resources. These measures, while essential to prevent breaches, may degrade user experience by increasing wait times or reducing throughput. Developers must reconcile the necessity of security with acceptable performance levels.

Consider the operation of secure data transmission as a case study illustrating the trade-off between security and performance. Encrypting data protects against interception and tampering but requires computational resources for both sender and receiver. The code snippet below simulates the encryption and decryption stages integrated into a data transfer process:

214

Table 9.6: *Strategies for Balancing Security and Performance*

Strategy	Security Impact	Performance Impact
Selective Encryption	Encrypt only sensitive fields or data segments	Reduces cryptographic workload, improves throughput
Hardware Acceleration	Use dedicated cryptographic hardware modules	High security with minimal CPU overhead
Session Key Caching	Reuse session keys within secured sessions	Decreases handshake frequency, lowers latency with controlled risk
Lazy Validation	Defer non-critical validation steps	May increase vulnerability window, speeds processing
Adaptive Security Levels	Adjust security protocols based on context or threat level	Balances protection with resource use dynamically

```
Original Data Size: 1 MB
Encryption Time: 150 ms
Transmission Time (unencrypted): 80 ms
Transmission Time (encrypted): 110 ms
Decryption Time: 150 ms
Total Secure Transfer Time: 410 ms
Total Unsecure Transfer Time: 80 ms
```

This output demonstrates that while encryption increases transfer time more than fivefold compared to unencrypted transmission, it provides essential confidentiality assurances. Accepting this overhead depends on the application's security requirements and performance constraints.

Approaches to balancing security and performance involve targeted optimizations that retain protective qualities while minimizing overhead. The table below compares various strategies:

Assessing risks involved in relaxing security for performance gains requires comprehensive evaluation of system vulnerabilities, threat models, and potential impacts. Performance-driven compromises must be justified with clear understanding of what threats may be introduced and mitigation plans. For instance, reducing encryption strength for speed might be acceptable for low-sensitivity data but not for financial transactions. Documenting decisions and performing periodic reassessments ensures compromises remain appropriate as contexts evolve.

Best practices for harmonizing security and performance recommend adopting architectural patterns that isolate security-critical operations from performance-critical paths. Middleware components can offload encryption and authentication to specialized services or hardware, minimizing the impact on core logic. Employing asynchronous processing for security tasks where possible prevents blocking user interactions. Secure coding standards and rigorous testing help detect vulnerabilities introduced by performance optimizations.

The following code example optimizes an authentication process by caching validated tokens to improve speed, while still verifying credentials upon expiry to preserve security integrity:

```
class Authenticator:
    def __init__(self):
        self.token_cache = {}
        self.token_expiry = 300  # seconds

    def authenticate(self, user_credentials):
        token = self.token_cache.get(user_credentials.user_id)
        current_time = get_current_time()
        if token and (current_time - token.creation_time) < self.
    token_expiry:
            return token  # Use cached token to speed up authentication

        # Perform full credential validation (slower path)
        if validate_credentials(user_credentials):
            new_token = generate_token(user_credentials.user_id)
            self.token_cache[user_credentials.user_id] = new_token
            return new_token
        else:
            raise AuthenticationError("Invalid credentials")
```

This approach reduces repeated expensive validations for successive requests while enforcing periodic re-validation to maintain security.

Mitigating risks introduced by performance optimizations includes implementing rate limiting to prevent brute force attacks exacerbated by caching or batching. Anomaly detection systems monitor for unusual activity patterns potentially enabled by altered execution paths. Ensuring strict access controls and sandboxing isolates components, reducing the impact of compromised modules. Adhering to the principle of least privilege and defense-in-depth further enhances security resilience without excessive performance sacrifice.

The interplay between security and performance necessitates careful, context-aware design decisions. Effective optimization involves recognizing unavoidable overheads of security functions and exploring complementary strategies such as hardware acceleration and selective protection. Continuous risk assessment, adherence to secure coding practices, and employing mitigation techniques enable developers to deliver systems that are concurrently secure and performant.

9.4   Builds and Compiler Optimization

Software development involves a critical phase known as building, where source code is translated into executable programs through compilation and linking. Understanding build configurations and compiler optimizations is essential for achieving efficient and maintainable software. Two primary build modes—debug and release—serve distinct purposes throughout the development lifecycle. Debug builds facilitate code inspection, error detection, and testing by incorporating debugging symbols and disabling aggressive optimizations. Release

Table 9.7: *Comparison of Debug and Release Builds*

Feature	Debug Build	Release Build
Debugging Symbols	Included	Usually omitted
Compiler Optimization Level	None or low (e.g., -O0)	High (e.g., -O2, -O3)
Execution Performance	Lower due to lack of optimization	Higher due to optimization techniques
Binary Size	Larger due to symbols and unoptimized code	Smaller after optimization and symbol removal
Compile Time	Faster (fewer optimizations)	Longer (complex optimizations)
Error Detection	Enhanced support for breakpoints, stack traces	Limited support, optimized code may inline or reorder

builds focus on maximizing runtime performance and minimizing binary size, enabling efficient deployment to end users.

The distinction between debug and release builds entails specific differences in compiler behavior, generated code, and auxiliary data retained within the binary. Debug builds typically include symbolic information mapping machine instructions back to source lines, supporting breakpoints and variable inspection in debuggers. Compiler optimizations are generally disabled or set to minimal levels to preserve code structure, ensuring a straightforward source-to-binary correspondence. In contrast, release builds activate a range of optimizations that restructure and streamline code for faster execution, smaller footprint, and improved utilization of processor features, often at the expense of debugger convenience.

The following table compares key characteristics of debug and release builds:

Compiler flags controlling optimization profoundly affect the generated executable's behavior. Common flags include -O0, -O1, -O2, and -O3, each enabling increasing levels of optimization. -O0 disables most

Table 9.8: *Comparison of Build Systems*

Tool	Primary Features	Typical Use Cases
Make	Simple dependency management via Makefiles, widely available	Small to medium C/C++ projects, legacy systems
CMake	Cross-platform generator for native build environments, supports complex builds	Multi-platform C/C++ projects, often combined with IDEs
Gradle	Incremental builds, dependency management, supports multiple languages	JVM and Android projects, multi-language complex systems
Bazel	High scalability, hermetic builds, parallel execution	Large codebases, monorepos, multi-language polyglot projects

optimizations, preserving code structure and facilitating debugging. -01 applies basic optimizations that improve performance without significantly complicating debugging. -02 activates a comprehensive set of optimizations balancing speed and code size, widely used in release builds. -03 enables aggressive optimizations such as inlining and loop unrolling, often yielding maximal performance but potentially increasing compile time and memory usage.

Beyond these, specialized flags tailor optimizations to target architectures or specific goals, such as -0s for size optimization or -0fast for ignoring strict standard compliance to gain speed. Selecting appropriate flags involves considering factors like debugging needs, target hardware, application requirements, and acceptable trade-offs.

Build tools orchestrate the compilation process, managing dependencies, configuration, and automation. Popular build systems include Make, CMake, Gradle, and Bazel, each offering varying features suited to different languages and project complexities. The table below summarizes their characteristics:

A typical command to compile a C++ source file with optimization flags might appear as follows:

```
g++ -std=c++17 -O2 -Wall -Wextra -o myprogram main.cpp utils.cpp
```

Here, -O2 instructs the compiler to perform standard optimizations, while -Wall and -Wextra enable additional warning messages to aid code quality.

The overall build process can be conceptualized as a series of distinct steps, outlined here in pseudocode serving as a flowchart description:

1: **Input:** Source code files
2: Parse build configuration files (Makefile, CMakeLists.txt, etc.)
3: Resolve dependencies and determine build order
4: **for all** source files **do**
5:     Preprocess source code (macro expansion, include files)
6:     Compile preprocessed code into object files
7: **end for**
8: Link object files into executable or library
9: Perform optional post-processing (strip symbols, packaging)
10: **Output:** Executable binary or library file

Build configurations influence runtime attributes significantly. Debug builds, prioritizing code analyzability, yield larger binaries with slower execution due to disabled optimizations and included symbols. Release builds produce compact, fast executables by reordering instructions, inlining functions, eliminating dead code, and applying other transformations. However, these transformations complicate debugging because source code lines may not correspond linearly to machine instructions, and some variables might be optimized away or stored in registers inaccessible to debuggers.

Selecting build options requires careful consideration of development objectives. During active coding and testing phases, using debug builds accelerates troubleshooting and improves error traceability. As code stabilizes, intermittent release builds verify performance characteristics and identify subtle optimization-related defects. Continuous integration systems often maintain separate pipelines for debug and release versions to automate validation. In production deployments, release builds ensure users receive responsive and resource-efficient software.

Best practices also advise managing build configurations systematically, leveraging tools like CMake to define compile-time options and external dependencies declaratively. Applying consistent naming conventions for build variants avoids confusion. Documentation of build settings and their intended use supports team collaboration. Profiling both debug and release builds helps identify discrepancies arising from optimization effects, guiding performance tuning. Using compiler-provided options for generating map files or intermediate outputs facilitates advanced analysis.

Effective build management and compiler optimization are foundational for delivering performant, maintainable software. Understanding the trade-offs between debug and release modes, judiciously applying optimization flags, and utilizing appropriate build tools empower developers to balance development efficiency, runtime performance, and robustness.

9.5 Real-World Case Studies

Performance optimization in software development often unfolds through iterative efforts responding to tangible challenges encountered in real-world applications. This section presents three concise case studies illustrating typical scenarios where targeted optimization significantly improved system responsiveness, energy efficiency, and throughput. These examples highlight common techniques and practical considerations, demonstrating how systematic analysis and adjustment can lead to substantial gains.

The first case study involves a web application suffering from high latency and slow page load times. The underlying issue stemmed primarily from inefficient database queries and the absence of effective caching strategies. Initial profiling revealed that repeated execution of complex queries caused bottlenecks, especially under high user load. By refactoring the queries to reduce unnecessary joins, introducing parameterized statements to improve execution plans, and implementing server-side caching of query results with expiration policies, the development team reduced average response times by over 50%. This not only enhanced user experience but also lowered database server load, thereby improving scalability and reliability.

In the second case study, a mobile application experienced rapid battery depletion attributed largely to frequent background activity and poorly optimized sensor usage. Optimization efforts concentrated on minimizing background processes by deferring non-essential synchronization tasks until the device was charging or connected to Wi-Fi. Additionally, hardware acceleration capabilities available on the target devices were leveraged for media decoding and graphics rendering, reducing CPU workload. Sensor polling rates were adjusted dynamically based on application state and user interaction, decreasing unnecessary sensor activations. These changes collectively extended average device battery life by approximately 30%, without compromising application functionality.

The third case study describes a data processing pipeline responsi-

222

Table **9.9**: *Normalized Performance Metrics Before and After Optimization*

Case Study	Before	After
Web Application Latency	1.0	0.48
Mobile App Battery Drain	1.0	0.70
Data Pipeline Processing	1.0	0.30

ble for large-scale analytics workloads. The pipeline initially employed naïve algorithms implemented in sequential code, resulting in prolonged processing times and inefficient resource use. By selecting more efficient algorithmic approaches—such as replacing nested loops with hash-based lookups and implementing early filtering—and porting compute-intensive sections to parallel execution using multithreading libraries, the team reduced processing time by nearly 70%. This acceleration enabled more frequent data refresh cycles and improved the responsiveness of downstream reporting systems.

Performance metrics documented before and after these optimizations illustrate tangible improvements. The table below, representing normalized latency or energy consumption relative to initial values, underscores the efficacy of the applied strategies:

These examples emphasize several lessons learned during the optimization processes. First, comprehensive profiling is indispensable for accurately identifying performance bottlenecks and focusing efforts effectively. Second, incremental changes targeting clear issues—such as query inefficiencies or unregulated background activity—yield measurable benefits. Third, exploiting hardware capabilities and modern programming paradigms like parallelism can unlock significant speedups. Fourth, balancing optimization with maintaining code clarity and functionality ensures sustainable development.

The tools and frameworks employed across these case studies varied

Table 9.10: *Frameworks and Tools Utilized in Optimization Case Studies*

Tool / Framework	Purpose	Applicable Case Study
SQL Profiler	Analyze and optimize database queries	Web Application
Redis Cache	Implement in-memory caching for fast data retrieval	Web Application
Android Profiler	Monitor battery usage, CPU, and network activity	Mobile App
OpenGL ES	Hardware-accelerated graphics rendering	Mobile App
Parallel Patterns Library (PPL)	Simplify parallelism in C++	Data Processing Pipeline
Linux perf	System-level profiling and performance measurement	Data Processing Pipeline

according to language and platform but shared a focus on facilitating measurement, analysis, and implementation of optimizations. The table below summarizes these technologies:

Optimization is inherently an iterative process necessitating repeated cycles of analysis and refinement. The workflow employed in these case studies can be represented in the following pseudocode outlining the essential stages:

1: Identify performance bottlenecks via profiling and monitoring
2: Analyze root causes and prioritize based on impact
3: Implement targeted optimizations addressing key issues
4: Verify performance gains through testing and benchmarking
5: **while** further improvements are possible **do**
6:      Continue refinement as necessary to meet goals
7: **end while**

This structured approach emphasizes measurement-driven decisions, avoiding premature or unfocused optimization efforts. Through continuous evaluation and thoughtful adjustment, software systems evolve toward greater efficiency and robustness, ultimately enhancing user satisfaction and operational effectiveness.

10

Best Practices and Key Takeaways

This chapter consolidates fundamental principles and practical advice for effective performance optimization. It emphasizes writing clear, maintainable, and efficient code as the foundation for long-term performance. The importance of leveraging existing libraries and avoiding premature optimization is highlighted to prevent unnecessary complexity. It advocates for continuous profiling, code reviews, and regression testing to sustain performance improvements across growing codebases. Overall, it provides a framework for adopting best practices that ensure scalable, reliable, and efficient software development.

10.1 Writing Clear, Maintainable, and Fast Code

Writing clear, maintainable, and efficient code constitutes the foundation for achieving sustainable program performance. Readability and structure are essential not only for initial development but also for facilitating future modifications, debugging, and optimization. Well-crafted code allows programmers to quickly understand functionality, identify performance bottlenecks, and apply improvements without introducing errors. Thus, clean code promotes long-term efficiency by minimizing technical debt and enabling systematic performance enhancements.

Central to readable code is the consistent use of meaningful naming conventions. Variables, functions, and classes should have descriptive, unambiguous names that communicate their purpose and content directly. Employing consistent naming patterns enhances code comprehension and reduces the cognitive load when navigating the codebase. For example, a variable holding the count of processed items might be named processedCount rather than a generic cnt or cryptic abbreviation. Functions should describe their actions clearly, such as calculateAverage or isValidInput, conveying intent precisely. Classes benefit from nouns or noun phrases reflecting their conceptual role, like UserAuthenticator or DataCache.

Equally important is adherence to uniform code formatting and style guidelines. These conventions govern indentation, spacing, line length, and comment placement to produce visually coherent and standardized source code. The table below summarizes common best practices for formatting that improve readability and reduce syntactical ambiguity.

Aspect	Guideline
Indentation	Consistent use of spaces or tabs (commonly 4 spaces per level) to visually separate code blocks.
Spacing	Include spaces around operators and after commas for clarity. Avoid excessive blank lines.
Line Length	Limit lines to 80–100 characters for easy scanning on various displays.
Braces	Place opening braces on the same line as control statements or function headers (consistent style).
Comments	Write concise, relevant comments above or beside complex or non-obvious code. Use block comments for section descriptions.
Naming Case	Use `camelCase` or `snake_case` consistently according to language conventions.

Table 10.1: *Summary of Common Code Formatting and Style Guidelines*

Comments and documentation enhance the communicative value of source code by explaining the rationale behind complex logic, describing inputs and outputs, and outlining assumptions or limitations. Effective comments clarify the purpose of code segments that are not immediately understandable from the code itself. However, comments should complement the code without restating obvious operations or becoming outdated. Proper documentation includes function headers with parameter descriptions, expected behavior, and return values; inline comments near intricate expressions; and module-level summaries defining the component's role in the system.

Refactoring is a disciplined practice of restructuring existing code to improve clarity without changing its external behavior. Identifying unclear or convoluted sections often requires detecting repeated code fragments, excessively long functions, deep nesting of control structures, or ambiguous variable names. The following pseudocode outlines a methodical approach to refactoring for clarity:

```
while codebase contains unclear code segments do
    identify code sections with poor readability or duplication
```

```
analyze logic to understand intended functionality
refactor code by:
    extracting smaller functions with descriptive names
    renaming variables and functions for clarity
    simplifying complex control flow (e.g., reduce nesting)
    removing redundant code or consolidating duplicates
    run tests to verify behavior remains unchanged
end while
```

Modular design supports code clarity and maintainability by dividing programs into small, focused units such as functions, classes, or modules. Each unit encapsulates specific responsibilities and exposes minimal interfaces. This separation aids understanding by allowing developers to concentrate on one logical component at a time. Additionally, modular components encourage code reuse and facilitate targeted testing. Modules with well-defined boundaries and single responsibilities reduce complexity and make refactoring or optimization safer and more manageable.

Avoiding code duplication is critical to reducing maintenance overhead and potential bugs. Redundant code fragments scattered throughout a project complicate updates, as a single change needs to be replicated in multiple locations. Techniques such as abstraction via functions or classes, and the use of reusable components, minimize repetition. Instead of copying and adapting code, programmers should identify common functionality and generalize it. This approach not only simplifies changes but also enhances overall code consistency, benefiting both readability and correctness.

Writing clean code does not mean ignoring performance considerations. In fact, well-structured and readable code enables easier identification of performance bottlenecks and facilitates efficient optimization. When code is tangled or unclear, pinpointing critical sections

230

that require tuning becomes onerous and error-prone. Clear separation of concerns and descriptive naming allow performance profiling tools and developers to focus analysis on the most impactful areas with confidence. Furthermore, clean code reduces the risk of premature or misguided optimizations that compromise maintainability.

Testing and validation serve as a foundation for maintaining correctness while pursuing code clarity and performance. Writing clear and maintainable unit tests verifies that code changes preserve functionality and aids early detection of regressions. Tests should be structured to isolate key behaviors and include assertions that confirm expected outcomes. Including performance checks, such as measuring execution times for critical functions, helps ensure that refactoring or new code additions do not degrade efficiency. The example below demonstrates a simple unit test verifying both correctness and reasonable performance of a sorting function.

```python
import time
import unittest

def sort_numbers(arr):
    return sorted(arr)

class TestSortNumbers(unittest.TestCase):
    def test_sort_correctness_and_speed(self):
        data = [5, 3, 1, 4, 2]
        start = time.time()
        result = sort_numbers(data)
        duration = time.time() - start
        self.assertEqual(result, [1, 2, 3, 4, 5])
        self.assertLess(duration, 0.01)  # Ensure fast execution

if __name__ == '__main__':
    unittest.main()
```

Maintaining this balance between clarity, maintainability, and performance empowers developers to build scalable and robust software systems. It ultimately leads to efficient workflows where code can be confidently improved over time without regressions or excessive complexity.

10.2 Leveraging Built-in Libraries and Functions

Utilizing built-in and well-tested libraries is a critical strategy in software development that supports both rapid implementation and reliable performance. Most modern programming languages provide extensive standard libraries covering a wide range of common operations, such as input/output handling, string manipulation, data structures, mathematical computations, and concurrency. These libraries have been developed and refined over many years by expert contributors, benefiting from rigorous testing, optimization, and compatibility adjustments. Relying on these preexisting components allows developers to avoid reinventing basic functionality and focus effort on domain-specific logic.

The advantages of using mature, well-supported libraries extend beyond convenience. Mature libraries significantly reduce the risk of bugs, since their code has been scrutinized and used extensively in diverse environments. The cumulative effect of this testing usually means fewer edge-case failures and unexpected behaviors compared to newly written code. Moreover, established libraries often include performance optimizations—such as algorithmic improvements and specialized implementations—that would be time-consuming and error-prone to reproduce independently. Thus, adopting these libraries improves both software reliability and efficiency.

The use of standard and third-party libraries also accelerates development timelines by providing ready-to-use solutions that are well documented and frequently maintained. Developers can leverage comprehensive APIs, examples, and community support, which further reduces the time needed to implement features correctly. Additionally, when a library is widely adopted, awareness of common pitfalls and effective usage patterns increases, enabling teams to integrate the tools with confidence.

The following table lists examples of commonly used libraries across several popular programming languages, illustrating their broad coverage of critical functionalities:

Language	Library	Purpose
Python	NumPy	Numerical array computations and linear algebra
Python	Pandas	Data manipulation and analysis
Python	requests	HTTP requests and networking
Python	tkinter	Basic graphical user interface components
Java	java.util	Collections framework, data structures, utilities
Java	java.nio	High-performance I/O and file handling
JavaScript	React	User interface building framework
JavaScript	Lodash	Utility functions for data manipulation
C++	STL (Standard Template Library)	Containers, iterators, algorithms
C++	Boost	Extended libraries for math, threading, networking

Table 10.2: *Examples of Common Libraries Across Languages*

Selecting the right library requires an evaluation of multiple factors to ensure that it aligns well with project requirements. Performance is often a primary consideration: the library should provide efficient implementations that meet expected throughput and latency targets. Beyond raw speed, community support and active maintenance are crucial for ensuring that bugs are addressed, compatibility with new language versions is maintained, and security vulnerabilities are remedied promptly. Compatibility with the existing codebase and deployment environment must also be verified, including licensing terms and integration complexity. Reading documentation, examining issue trackers, and consulting developer forums help gauge the maturity and suitability of a library.

To demonstrate practical use, consider this example showcasing efficient array operations using the widely adopted NumPy library in Python. NumPy exploits low-level optimizations and vectorized operations, resulting in significant speed advantages over basic Python loops.

```
import numpy as np

# Create a large array of random numbers
data = np.random.rand(1000000)

# Compute the mean efficiently using NumPy's optimized function
mean_value = np.mean(data)

print(f"Mean of data: {mean_value}")
```

Such usage contrasts sharply with naïve implementations that iterate over elements in Python, highlighting the performance benefits of leveraging specialized libraries designed for heavy computation.

Before fully adopting any library, it is prudent to benchmark its performance relative to project needs. Benchmarking involves systematic measurement of execution times, memory usage, and throughput under representative workloads. Automated benchmarking frameworks or custom test scripts can facilitate this process. Comparing multiple candidate libraries or implementations helps identify the best match for performance criteria. Profiling library functions during normal operation also aids in understanding their impact on overall system efficiency.

Effective integration of libraries requires attention to dependency management. Version control tools and package managers assist in specifying exact library versions to ensure reproducibility. Establishing procedures for updating dependencies while verifying backward compatibility helps avoid unexpected regressions. Minimizing dependency bloat by including only necessary libraries reduces build size and potential attack surfaces. Clear documentation of all third-party components and their licenses supports maintainability and legal compliance.

Despite their advantages, external libraries carry potential risks. Excessive reliance on many libraries can lead to dependency bloat, increasing binary size and complicating update cycles. Some libraries may introduce security vulnerabilities either through outdated code or insufficient scrutiny. Unmaintained libraries risk incompatibility with new platforms or languages. Careful evaluation of library health, periodic security audits, and timely updates mitigate these risks. When possible, prefer libraries with active development communities and transparent governance.

The value of adopting well-tested frameworks is illustrated by the following example case study. A development team transitioned a web application from handcrafted data handling to using the mature Django framework in Python. This adoption resulted in measurable performance improvements and a reduction in bugs due to the integrated caching, ORM optimizations, and rigorous framework testing. The output below summarizes key benefits observed post-integration.

```
Case Study: Django Framework Adoption
-------------------------------------
- Request handling latency decreased by 30%
- Number of reported bugs related to database access dropped by 45%
- Development velocity improved through reusable components
- Security vulnerabilities reduced with built-in protections
```

This example demonstrates how selecting a reliable, established framework can positively influence both performance and code quality, confirming the advantages of leveraging existing solutions when appropriate.

Incorporating well-tested libraries and frameworks is a fundamental practice for achieving robust, efficient, and maintainable software. Thorough evaluation, benchmarking, and careful integration ensure that these tools contribute positively without introducing undue risk. By focusing development effort on novel and application-specific logic rather than reinventing core functionality, programmers create higher-quality software with improved performance characteristics over time.

10.3   Avoiding Premature Optimization

Premature optimization refers to the practice of attempting to improve the performance of code before there is clear evidence that such improvements are necessary or effective. This approach often arises from the instinctive desire to write fast code from the outset or to anticipate future performance demands without concrete data. While performance tuning is an essential aspect of software development, optimizing too early in the process can introduce significant risks and inefficiencies that outweigh the potential benefits. Understanding the pitfalls of premature optimization and adopting data-driven strategies ensures that development resources are focused effectively and that code remains maintainable and clear.

The costs associated with early optimization extend beyond wasted developer time. Premature tuning frequently results in overly complex and convoluted code that is difficult to read, maintain, and extend. Efforts to enhance performance without a full understanding of actual bottlenecks may lead to intricate algorithms or low-level tricks that obscure the original program logic. This complexity increases the likelihood of bugs and reduces overall code quality. Additionally, time spent optimizing inconsequential code paths diverts effort from core functionality, testing, and usability improvements. Thus, premature optimization can inadvertently degrade the long-term viability and reliability of software projects.

Effective performance optimization begins with profiling: the systematic measurement and analysis of code execution to identify areas that have the greatest impact on overall speed or resource consumption. Profiling provides objective data, pinpointing critical bottlenecks rather than subjective guesses. By quantifying where time or memory is concentrated, developers gain actionable insights that inform targeted and justified optimizations. Without such evidence, efforts risk focusing on parts of the program that contribute little to the actual performance, yielding negligible improvements despite substantial effort.

The table below illustrates a hypothetical comparison between optimization effort and actual performance gains for various code sections, emphasizing the importance of evidence-based tuning.

Code Section	Optimization Effort (hours)	Speedup (%)	Comment
Data Parsing	2	5	Minor impact on total runtime; not critical
File I/O	5	30	Significant bottleneck; worthwhile optimization
UI Rendering	8	10	Limited effect; complex and fragile code
Algorithm Calculation	12	50	Major hotspot; gave excellent speed improvements
Logging	1	0	Optimization yielded no measurable gains

Table 10.3: *Optimization Effort vs. Performance Gain: Evidence-Based Focus*

Common pitfalls arising from premature optimization include focusing on uncritical code paths, sacrificing code clarity for marginal gains, and inadvertently introducing bugs. For example, developers might attempt micro-optimizations such as using manual loop unrolling or complex bitwise operations in parts of the code executed infrequently or that do not dominate runtime. Such changes increase code complexity and maintenance burden with little net benefit. Similarly, replacing readable straightforward code with cryptic equivalents can obstruct future debugging and extension, thereby harming overall software quality. In some cases, careless optimizations cause subtle defects or security issues that propagate unnoticed.

The following code snippet exemplifies a premature optimization pitfall: unnecessary micro-optimizations complicate simple logic without delivering meaningful improvements.

```
# Inefficient attempt at micro-optimization
```

```
def sum_squares(nums):
    result = 0
    for i in range(len(nums)):
        n = nums[i]
        # Using bitwise operators unnecessarily
        result += (n << 1) * (n >> 1)
    return result
```

In contrast, a clear and direct implementation, such as `result += n * n`, both expresses intent plainly and likely performs as well or better with modern compiler optimizations.

Best practice dictates establishing a performance baseline through profiling before undertaking tuning. This workflow involves measuring system behavior, identifying true bottlenecks, and prioritizing optimization efforts on those code regions where improvements will have significant impact. By adhering to this approach, development teams avoid wasted effort and maintain code clarity. The process also facilitates regression detection, ensuring that performance gains are validated and no unintended degradations occur.

A systematic iterative optimization strategy can be summarized in the following pseudocode flowchart:

```
REPEAT
    PROFILE the application to gather performance data
    IDENTIFY critical bottlenecks based on metrics
    OPTIMIZE selected hotspots in code, preserving clarity
    RE-PROFILE to validate improvement and check for regressions
UNTIL performance goals are met or further gains are negligible
```

This cycle promotes incremental enhancements informed by evidence and maintains a balance between speed and maintainability.

Maintaining clear, readable code is paramount even when applying optimizations. Optimization should be targeted and conservative, avoid-

ing large-scale rewrites that obscure logic unless the performance benefit justifies the complexity cost. Clear naming, modular design, and
comprehensive testing remain essential to sustaining long-term software quality. Comments explaining the reasons for specific optimizations assist future maintainers in understanding trade-offs made during development. Ultimately, balancing readability and performance
ensures that software remains practical to evolve and adapt while delivering efficient execution.

By resisting the urge to optimize prematurely and committing to an empirical, measured development process, programmers produce codebases that are both performant and maintainable. This disciplined
approach leads to more predictable outcomes and higher-quality software over the entire lifecycle.

10.4   Sustaining Performance in Growing Code-bases

Maintaining high performance in software over time requires more
than one-time optimizations; it demands deliberate, ongoing strategies that adapt to continuous code changes and evolving project requirements. As codebases grow in size and complexity, new features,
bug fixes, and refactoring can inadvertently degrade performance. Sustainable performance management involves integrating practices that
detect regressions early, track performance trends, and reinforce best
practices throughout the development lifecycle. Such proactive measures ensure that software remains efficient, responsive, and resource-
conscious as it matures.

One fundamental tool in sustaining performance is the practice of code reviews with an explicit focus on performance considerations. Regular peer reviews allow developers to evaluate changes for their potential impact on runtime efficiency, memory usage, and scalability. Reviewers can identify patterns that often cause bottlenecks, such as inefficient loops, excessive object creation, or blocking operations. They also promote adherence to established performance guidelines and architectural principles. Code reviews foster collective ownership of performance quality, facilitating knowledge sharing and reducing the likelihood of inadvertent regressions slipping into the codebase.

Continuous profiling plays a central role in ongoing performance management by providing real-time or periodic measurement of application behavior in production or staging environments. Various tools and techniques enable developers to capture detailed metrics such as CPU usage, memory consumption, I/O wait times, and response latency. The table below compares several popular continuous profiling tools and approaches, illustrating their suitability for different environments and analysis needs.

Tool	Type	Features and Use Cases
perf	Linux system profiler	Low-level CPU profiling; suitable for native applications
Valgrind	Instrumentation framework	Memory profiling and leak detection; developer environment
Flamegraph	Visualization tool	Visual representation of call stacks and hotspots
Prometheus	Metrics collection	Time-series metrics with alerting for web services
Jaeger	Distributed tracing	Tracks request flows and latency across microservices
Py-Spy	Sampling profiler for Python	Low-overhead profiling in production

Table 10.4: *Comparison of Continuous Profiling Tools and Techniques*

These tools enable teams to observe the real-world performance characteristics of their software continuously, uncovering regressions or inefficiencies introduced by new code or changing workloads.

Regression testing is an essential complement to continuous profiling, focusing on preventing performance degradations as code evolves. Automated test suites incorporating performance benchmarks verify that critical functions meet defined speed or memory usage targets before integration. By embedding performance assertions in the testing process, teams ensure that changes do not inadvertently slow down application components or increase resource consumption. Such tests are typically run on continuous integration servers, providing rapid feedback to developers and enabling quick remediation of performance issues.

Monitoring key performance metrics over time provides valuable insight into the health and evolution of software systems. Visualization of data such as request latency, throughput, CPU load, and memory usage across multiple releases helps identify trends, regressions, or improvements. The example below shows a graph tracking average response time over several software versions, illustrating the detection of a performance regression followed by corrective intervention.

```
Response Time Over Releases
+-----------------------------------------------+
| Release |          Avg Response Time (ms)     |
|-----------------------------------------------|
| 1.0     | 120
| 1.1     | 125
| 1.2     | 150  <-- Regression detected
| 1.3     | 130  <-- Optimized fix deployed
| 1.4     | 125
+-----------------------------------------------+
```

Such monitoring enables data-driven decision making and prioritizes performance work within the development backlog.

To integrate performance practices smoothly into development work-flows, teams should adopt best practices that combine profiling, test-ing, and code review seamlessly. Establishing performance budgets for critical metrics guides both developers and reviewers to maintain target thresholds. Automating performance tests alongside functional tests ensures consistent enforcement. Documentation outlining com-mon performance anti-patterns and recommended alternatives edu-cates the team. Encouraging open communication about performance implications promotes a culture attentive to efficiency. Together, these measures embed performance as a core quality attribute rather than an afterthought.

The following real-world example illustrates how a development team sustained and improved performance in an evolving codebase. Ini-tially encountering increased page load latency after adding new an-alytics features, the team used continuous profiling tools to identify an expensive synchronous database query as the source. By refactor-ing the query to be asynchronous and caching results, they reduced latency and CPU usage. Regular regression tests confirmed the im-provements and prevented reintroduction of similar bottlenecks in fu-ture updates.

- Issue detected: 25% increase in page load time (v2.5)

- Profiling identified blocking DB query on user metrics

- Optimization: Converted query to asynchronous with caching

- Result: Latency decreased by 30%, CPU usage down by 15%

- Regression tests included to prevent recurrence

- Performance review integrated into sprint retrospectives

This case illustrates the benefits of combining monitoring, profiling, testing, and team coordination in maintaining software responsiveness over time.

The process of sustained performance optimization can be summarized in the following iterative workflow:

```
LOOP
    MEASURE system performance using profiling and metrics
    ANALYZE data to identify regressions or bottlenecks
    OPTIMIZE identified hotspots with targeted code changes
    VALIDATE effectiveness via regression tests and benchmarks
    DOCUMENT findings and update performance guidelines
END LOOP
```

This repeatable cycle institutionalizes continuous attention to performance, enabling teams to manage growth without sacrificing efficiency or user experience.

By embracing these integrated practices, development teams ensure that software performance remains robust despite ongoing evolution. Proactive detection and timely remediation of performance issues avoid costly problems in production and reduce technical debt. Ultimately, sustainable performance management contributes to delivering resilient, scalable, and user-friendly applications throughout their lifecycle.

10.5   Summary and Glossary

Consolidating the key concepts and terminology presented throughout this chapter is essential for reinforcing understanding and providing a reliable reference for future study. Clear definitions and a synthesized overview assist readers in connecting individual topics into a coherent framework. This section reviews the most important points addressed, recapitulating foundational ideas essential for effective performance optimization, and supplies a glossary to clarify terminology commonly encountered in this domain.

The chapter has emphasized that writing clear, maintainable, and fast code is the cornerstone of sustainable software performance. Readability and structure facilitate ongoing enhancements and simplify identification of performance bottlenecks. Leveraging built-in and well-tested libraries accelerates development and improves reliability, while also offering optimized implementations that are difficult to reproduce independently. Avoiding premature optimization prevents unnecessary complexity and misdirected effort by focusing performance improvements on evidence-supported bottlenecks discovered through profiling. Sustaining performance in growing codebases demands continual attention via code reviews, continuous profiling, regression testing, and monitoring, ensuring that new code additions do not degrade system efficiency over time.

Presented below is a glossary table summarizing important terms related to performance optimization, aiming to clarify fundamental vocabulary for reference.

Term	Definition
Profiling	The process of measuring program execution characteristics to identify performance bottlenecks.
Big O Notation	A mathematical notation that describes the upper bound of an algorithm's complexity in terms of input size.
Cache Locality	The property that data items accessed close together in time are also stored close together in memory, optimizing CPU cache usage.
Premature Optimization	The act of optimizing code before sufficient evidence of performance issues exists, often leading to inefficiency and complexity.
Regression Testing	Automated tests designed to catch functional or performance degradations after code changes.
Modular Design	The architectural practice of decomposing software into independent, encapsulated components.
Benchmarking	Systematic testing to measure and compare the performance of various code or components.
Code Review	A peer examination of source code to ensure correctness, readability, and adherence to standards, including performance considerations.
Dependency Bloat	The inclusion of excessive external libraries or components that increase software size and complexity.
Latency	The delay between initiating a task and its completion or visible response in a system.

Table 10.5: *Glossary of Key Terms in Performance Optimization*

Cache locality refers to the tendency of programs to access data elements that are near each other in memory within a short period. Effective cache locality reduces cache misses, enabling faster data retrieval from CPU caches instead of slower main memory. Optimizing data structures and access patterns to improve cache locality enhances overall program speed.

Big O notation characterizes the growth rate of an algorithm's running time or space requirements relative to input size. It allows programmers to estimate the efficiency of algorithms by classifying them into categories such as $O(1)$ constant time, $O(n)$ linear time, or $O(n \log n)$ logarithmic time complexity, guiding informed algorithm selection.

- Profile first to identify true bottlenecks before making optimization decisions.

- Write clear, maintainable, and modular code to enable easier debugging and future improvements.

- Leverage existing, well-tested libraries and functions for reliable and efficient implementations.

- Avoid premature optimization that sacrifices readability and introduces complexity without evidence of need.

- Employ continuous profiling and regression testing to detect and prevent performance regressions.

- Integrate performance considerations into code reviews and development workflows.

- Measure and monitor performance metrics consistently throughout the software lifecycle.

- Use benchmarking to compare alternative approaches quantitatively.

- Balance trade-offs between speed, memory usage, maintainability, and security mindfully.

- Document performance-related decisions and maintain clear communication within development teams.

Deepening one's understanding of performance optimization benefits from practical experience, ongoing study, and engagement with the programming community. Experimenting with profiling tools and benchmarking frameworks on real projects develops intuition for spotting bottlenecks. Reading research and case studies exposes learners to advanced techniques and diverse optimization scenarios. Participating in forums, code reviews, and conferences facilitates knowledge exchange and keeps practitioners informed about evolving best practices and emerging tools. Establishing continuous learning habits is key to mastering performance optimization in a rapidly changing technological landscape.

By consolidating and referencing this chapter's critical concepts and terminology, readers gain a durable foundation to approach performance challenges methodically. The principles outlined here support writing software that remains efficient, maintainable, and scalable as it evolves, ensuring robust outcomes in both individual projects and collaborative development environments.